The Parwan Wind
Dust Motes

The Parwan Wind
Dust Motes

B.K. Zahrah Nasir

Introduction by
Muneeza Shamsie

OXFORD
UNIVERSITY PRESS

OXFORD
UNIVERSITY PRESS

Great Clarendon Street, Oxford OX2 6DP

Oxford University Press is a department of the University of Oxford.
It furthers the University's objective of excellence in research, scholarship,
and education by publishing worldwide in

Oxford New York

Auckland Cape Town Dar es Salaam Hong Kong Karachi
Kuala Lumpur Madrid Melbourne Mexico City Nairobi
New Delhi Shanghai Taipei Toronto

with offices in

Argentina Austria Brazil Chile Czech Republic France Greece
Guatemala Hungary Italy Japan Poland Portugal Singapore
South Korea Switzerland Turkey Ukraine Vietnam

Oxford is a registered trade mark of Oxford University Press
in the UK and in certain other countries

ISBN 978-0-19-547402-2

Cover Design by K.B. Abro

Typeset in Times
Printed in Pakistan by
Namaa Lica Printers, Karachi.
Published by
Ameena Saiyid, Oxford University Press
No. 38, Sector 15, Korangi Industrial Area, PO Box 8214
Karachi-74900, Pakistan.

CONTENTS

CONTENTS

LIST OF PHOTOGRAPHS

Between pp. 32 to 33

All photographs courtesy B.K. Zahrah Nasir

1. Commander M. Anwar, Jegdalek, 1983.
2. Mohammad Anwar Jekdalek, 2004.
3. Commander Gul Ruz, Tora Ara, 1983.
4. Commander Gul Ruz, 2004.
5. Rubina Mqueir.
6. Friba Rezzai.
7. Darwish.
8. Farhad
9. America meets Kabul.
10. An incredible swimming pool.
11. Reservoir, Bagh-e-Babur.
12. Babur's tomb.
13. The Mausoleum of King Nadir Shah.
14. Shipping container stores.
15. Darulaman Palace.
16. Kargha Lake.

ACKNOWLEDGEMENTS

First and foremost I would like to thank my husband, Ali Azhar Nasir, for his patience, support and understanding both when I visited Afghanistan and then during the long hours of writing when he has often been left to do the cooking!

This book would not have been possible without the co-operation of M. Anwar Jekdalek, Commander Gul Ruz, Farhad and all the other people, old friends and new, who spent their time explaining the current situation in Kabul to me when they had so many other, far more important, things on their agendas.

A big thank you goes out to Fatima and Fateh Ali Vellani for literally forcing me into the world of computers, which despite my initial reservations, has proved to be extremely helpful indeed especially with my 'Techi', Zunaira Durrani, to guide me through the various technological problems I continue to encounter.

Asma Wajahat deserves a hug for her comments on the original manuscript and encouragement thereafter, and I wait, with baited breath, to see what type of book she will undoubtedly write in the future. A best-seller I hope!

Family and friends, too numerous to mention have also been very supportive throughout this project.

Last, but by no means least Jean Bambrick for kick-starting my writing career and the team at Oxford University Press in Karachi who have maintained faith in my work...long may they continue to do so.

Thank you all!

B.K. Zahrah Nasir
Bhurban
Pakistan

INTRODUCTION

By *Muneeza Shamsie*

It roars out of the Paghman mountains north of Kabul.
Rampages across the province which bears its name to whistle through
this tortured city.
It lowers the temperature and raises the dust.
I am sure it can drive people insane
       – *The Parwan Wind—Dust Motes* by B.K. Zahrah Nasir

These words by B.K. Zahrah Nasir provide the central metaphor for
The Parwan Wind—Dust Motes a book about her visit to Afghanistan
in 2004 in which she gathers up and scatters across her narrative many
stories of dispersal, survival and suffering, in a series of anecdotes,
i.e. 'Dust Motes'. The Scottish-born Zahrah Nasir is no stranger to
Afghanistan. Her previous trip there in 1983, is the subject of her first
book, *The Gun Tree* which provides an account of what is an
extraordinary experience for any woman to have passed through.

The Scottish born Zahrah Nasir, or Pam Morris, as she then was,
is one of the very few women, to have participated in the war with
the *Mujahideen*, albeit for a brief period of ten days. In *The Gun Tree*,
she wrote with hindsight 'I was already verging on insanity when I
undertook the journey. I needed to feel this sharp edge, experience
shock and fear, in order to shed my manacles and walk free'.[1]

At that time, Pam Morris was 27 years old. She had been a battered
wife, lost the custody of her children and was on the edge of a
breakdown. However, adventure books and the very word
'Afghanistan' had always fascinated her. She joined *The Inverness
Courier* as a journalist, sold her few possessions and dashed off to
'make contact with the Mujahideen, the Afghan resistance fighters,
and go with them to fight the Russians.'[2] The *Mujahideen* commander
did not want to speak to her, let alone take her across the border. He
created many impediments. She kept up with his troops on foot, half-
running, half walking across rugged mountains, until he said: 'Yes,

you can walk. You have Afghan muscles but you are a woman and here is a horse for you.'[3] He also noticed that she did not balk or flee, in the midst of thundering *Mujahideen* Kalashnikovs while Russian reconnaissance planes flew overhead and Russian helicopters circled threateningly low. She knew she could not afford to show weakness. She wrote: 'While the *Mujahideen* accepted me as a strong woman, one who could walk or ride with them, there would be no problems.' The minute I transformed into a soft, vulnerable female, I was in trouble.[4]

The Afghans named her Banafsha-Khomar. She rode with them, veiled. She experienced fear, hunger, and exhaustion—sometimes travelling 23 hours in a day. She used powerful guns. She saw bombs fall and people die. She looked on with horror, because there were no medicines for the wounded and maimed. At the base camp, she was the only woman among 1,500 men. In that unlikely terrain, among strangers, she found that for the first time in her life, she was accepted for herself, as a person, regardless of gender. In *The Gun Tree* she records how this enabled her to find her sense of self. But for a young woman, to have earned the respect and trust of the *Mujahideen*, in that all-male world of hardened, fighting troops, is surely exceptional.

The Gun Tree is a sparse, passionate book, a combination of narrative, free verse and diary, which became immensely topical after the events of 9/11. The title was taken from the mulberry tree on which the Mujahideen hung their guns. However, the commander sent her away, back to Pakistan, the day he feared his base camp would be bombed. The book culminates with Zahrah Nasir's return to Scotland and her great disappointment that the western world had other pre-occupations and did not want to hear about what she had seen in Afghanistan, the country in which she converted to Islam.

All this contributed to her sense of alienation in Scotland. She moved to Oman, where she met and married a Pakistani. She lives in Bhurban now, amid Pakistan's pine-clad mountains and is also well known for her weekly gardening column in *Dawn*.

The Parwan Wind is a more intricate, cohesive and substantial work than *The Gun Tree*; it carries the narrative forward but also welds past and present, juxtaposing memories and images of 1983, with observations of Afghanistan today. All this has a resonance far beyond

Afghanistan: it makes a telling comment on the high ideals of 'The Cause', the heroism and terrors of War, the frightening ambiguities and compromises of Peace; it spells out exactly what it means, for any country, to have gone through such an uncompromising experience. The book also fills in the silences of *The Gun Tree*, including locations, places, people she had not named originally, for security reasons.

In *The Parwan Wind*, Zahrah Nasir reveals that the 1983 base camp she stayed at, was in Jegdalek. The commander was Gul Ruz of the Jamiat-i-Islami, Afghanistan. His companions included the charismatic Commander Anwar, now a man holding high office in Kabul. She also says she embarked on her 2004 journey to Afghanistan, uncertain of what she would find. She had no idea how many of her *Mujahideen* friends were still live, or what had become of Commander Gul Ruz.

The Parwan Wind begins with a whirl of memories and romantic images from that distant time—mountains and cornflowers, 'proud faces, bandoliers of bullets, Kalashnikovs', voices calling her 'Banafsha-Khomar, Banafsha-Khomar'. The hard realities of a people, rich or poor, half-hoping to reclaim old certainties, trying to cope with endless tragedies and coming to terms with the present, begins at the airport with Zahrah Nasir's first 'Dust Mote'. She tells of her conversation with a rich, well-educated, hazel-eyed young woman, who has spent years of exile in Europe, the Middle East, India and Pakistan, but is coming back to Kabul from her job as a financial consultant in Germany to help her country. Her father, a religious leader and other men of the family, including her grandfather, were taken away by the Communists during the Saur Revolution and never seen again.

This combination of tragedy, brutality, dislocation, reclamation and hope, runs through many of the stories that Zahrah Nasir records in Kabul 'a city struggling to rise from the ashes'. In the streets there are armed patrols and 'doomed houses'; there is also an overgrown golf course and a huge palace reduced to a 'haunted shell'. Perhaps nothing encapsulates the recent history and scars of Kabul better than Zahrah Nasir's description of Babur's tomb and its gardens:

Infighting between the Mujahideen was responsible for much of the garden's destruction, as were later predations by the Taliban who 'massacred' the ancient *chinar* trees standing between Babur's tomb and the delicate marble mosque, built by Emperor Shah Jahan in 1645, close by. The civil war destroyed the pavilion, exposing the tomb to the elements again, as Babur had wished, but it also destroyed the beautiful mosque which is now being painstakingly recreated.

Foreign powers such as the Russians, Americans and Pakistanis have all added to the maelstrom and the savagery; Dostum, Rabbani, Massoud, Hekmatyar, Mullah Omar among others, are all responsible for excesses or crimes, to a greater or lesser degree. Walking through the famous stadium, where the Taliban committed terrible deeds in the name of justice, God and religion, Zahrah Nasir recalls:

> I try not to imagine the numberless amputations, the executions which took place here.
> Try not to picture the blood.
> The ghosts of Taliban victims scream at me in anguish.

In Kabul, Zahrah Nasir is welcomed by Commander Anwar, now Mr Anwar Jekdalek, 'a rather urbane, middle aged 'gentleman'.... greying hair, bald spot, reading glasses'. He is a man of considerable importance. He is watched over by bodyguards and has spokesmen at his side. Zahrah Nasir is in Kabul to interview him, though he proves rather elusive. She has met him at various intervals since the base camp at Jegdalek in 1983. In a Peshawar refugee camp, his parents welcomed her as their daughter. Years later, they presented her with rich wedding gifts as 'family', because she was newly married, although they were in mourning for their murdered son, Arif.

But in 1994 Anwar suddenly turned up in Scotland. He bombarded Zahrah Nasir with questions. 'Why were you in Peshawar?' 'What do you know about Arif? His murder? 'How many times have you been to Afghanistan?' In Kabul 2004, he remains an enigma, a man who is as unsure of her, as she is of him. When she tries to photograph him he turns 'a sickly kind of green'. Suddenly Zahrah Nasir realizes that he fears she might assassinate him. He 'is remembering what happened to Ahmed Shah Massoud. Guns and bombs hidden inside journalists cameras'. For him—and so many others—suspicion is self-preservation, a way of life. At the same time, Anwar will not hear of Zahrah Nasir staying anywhere in Kabul, except with his family—

namely, his nephew, Farhad. Through Farhad and his fiancé, the book provides a glimpse into the lives of a younger generation: political exile, personal tragedy, a childhood spent, partly or entirely, in a refugee camp or some distant, foreign land, an uneasy homecoming.

One of the most entertaining passages in the book describes the Afghan wedding that Zahrah Nasir attends. There she discovers she is the only woman in traditional Afghan dress. The attire of the others ranges 'from Madhuri Dixit to Scarlett O'Hara'. There are Bollywood-type saris, bright Punjabi *joras*, *ghararas*, *sharararas*, long Victorian or Edwardian style dresses. She has already discovered that the women of Afghanistan are very different to the 'shadowy, *burkha*-clad figures' she had expected to see. She comments:

> I was stunned to see young women wearing long skirts, fashionably slit to the knee, exposing white *shalwars*, or the more daring, 1950s style fishnet stockings. ... Others wear bell-bottomed trousers or jeans and jackets.

Zahrah Nasir also realized, very soon, that the citified people of Kabul are very different to the tribal Afghans she has previously met in Jegdalek.

At the heart of her narrative there is Commander Gul Ruz, her onetime hero and protector. To her, he seems 'totally out of place, out of time... a mountain man come to the city.' He is also older, wearier. Instead of a horse, he has 'a travel stained Toyota Corolla'. His second wife, lives with him in a Kabul apartment—his first wife lives in the village. There is a sudden glimpse of him as a family man—a father of twelve children—six from each wife. He is a man, as large as life, open, warm and hospitable, a marked contrast to his enigmatic and powerful friend, Anwar Jekdalek. Urban, modern Kabul hardly seems to contain Gul Ruz. However, he is still a soldier, a Commander in the Afghan army. His eldest son, who was 13 in Jegdalek, serves in the same regiment as him, but speaks English, Urdu, Dari and Pashto. This multi-lingual young man acts as the translator between Gul Ruz and Zahrah Nasir, as Gul Ruz tells his story, from his years as a farmer to *Mujahideen* commander, and his entry into Kabul in 1992, when the Russians left: he naively thought then, that the war was over. But the *Mujahideen* fought each other until they were ousted by the

Taliban in 1996. Gul Ruz retreated to Panjshir with Ahmed Shah Massoud; he and some of his family hid and lived in caves until the American intervention and a new government enabled Gul Ruz to return to Kabul

Zahrah Nasir's interview with Gul Ruz touches at the very heart of Afghanistan and its devastation, after a prolonged, ferocious civil war. She tries to remind Gul Ruz, that the freedom Afghanistan has attained amid such a palpable foreign presence is not that which he fought for, but he prevaricates, becomes irritated and refuses to accept such an idea. She laments:

> ... the fighting still continues, remnants of the Taliban and other malcontents, carrying out more and more attacks on both foreign occupation forces and the newly re-formed Afghan Army and police forces. No matter how long and hard one looks into the tangled web of Afghan and foreign intrigue, there is still no actual peace in sight.

In *The Parwan Wind*, as Zahrah Nasir relates many other moving stories, she also realizes that the Afghanistan, which had beckoned to her in her imagination, for all those years, no longer exists. There remain too many disturbing questions, too many uncertainties, too much brutalization. Her love and sympathy for the land never wavers, however. She provides a rare and unusual insight into Afghan life today and to the struggles, hopes and aspirations of its people. Here is a story, not about grand political designs, but individual lives which embody the collection and describe exactly what it means to have survived and lived through such great, armed upheavals across three decades. And there is a clear moral to her story: it is time that the countries, who have thought of their Afghan involvement as a new 'Great Game'—that fictitious, erroneous term, spawned by colonial storytellers—took a long hard look at the cost of their deeds and their tragic consequences.

NOTES

1. B.K. Zahrah Nasir, *The Gun Tree* (Karachi: Oxford University Press, 2001).
2. Ibid.
3. Ibid.
4. Ibid.

INTRODUCTION

Making a return trip to Afghanistan was always on the cards for me.

To be honest...it couldn't be otherwise.

I had both left an integral part of myself there when I travelled with the *Mujahideen* way back in 1983, and, more importantly from a personal point of view, emerged from my experiences then as the embryo of the person I find myself to be now.

Being closely involved in any war is probably more than enough to alter anyone's perspective and my days in the mountains of Afghanistan with the *Mujahideen* as they fought Soviet occupation certainly changed life for me.

For some unknown reason, I felt myself to have become 'bonded' with the courageous men and women I met at that time and there was always an unwritten understanding that I would return...though none of us, neither they nor I, expected a full twenty-one years to pass until I set foot on Afghan soil once more.

The reasons for the delay are manifold; changes within Afghanistan itself, changes in my own personal situation, from single to married, from Scotland to the Sultanate of Oman, back to Scotland and then to Pakistan, settling first in Karachi and then moving to the mountains of Bhurban where we currently reside.

Mountains have a lot to do with my life.

I cannot settle without them.

I am a mountain person at heart.

Mountains and my own home and land...this is the total sum of my security!

It is what I am content with and what I thought the *Mujahideen*, my *Mujahideen* anyway, were fighting for when I first met them.

I had kept in touch with some of the people I wrote about, but did not then name, in my previous book *The Gun Tree*...a very short attempt at narrating a personal experience of that momentous time for all who were caught up in it.

Correspondence was rather sporadic and actual face-to-face meetings extremely few and far between, taking place as they did in London, Peshawar and then on my previous home territory in Scotland.

During the '*Taliban* time' we drifted completely out of touch and it wasn't until after they fell from power that I once again came across the name of Mohammad Anwar, one of the *Mujahideen* commanders I had previously travelled with.

His name was in a newspaper report about conditions in Kabul in 2002.

I was not at all surprised to learn that he was 'Mayor of Kabul' and had been for sometime.

Finding a way to re-establish contact with him though was quite another matter.

There was no postal system as such, no telephone system either.

The Afghan Embassy in Islamabad couldn't help...at first...but finally came through two long years later after I had discovered that Mohammad Anwar was, and is, also the President of the Olympic Committee of Afghanistan and when a group of Afghan athletes were coming to Pakistan to participate in the SAARC Games of 2004.

I had wondered if Mohammad Anwar would accompany them.

He didn't but an immediate associate of his did.

Contact was established.

I was invited to Kabul to visit and made my travel plans, after convincing my long suffering husband that I would be safe and secure, accordingly.

Kabul.

One of the most dangerous cities on earth.

I had never been there before.

Cities are not my thing.

I wished that I could return to the mountainous area of Jegdalek, walk where I had previously done so, sit underneath '*The Gun Tree*' once more, this time in peace not war.

Unfortunately this was, and still is, impossible as remnants of the *Taliban* have regrouped in that locality, also, the entire valley is full of mines.

I had a need to know and understand what had happened to all of my 'friends' in the intervening years.

To learn from their experiences…if they would tell me.

To know if they had won whatever it was they had been fighting for.

Going to Kabul to meet Mohammad Anwar was all that I could do.

It was a first step at least.

I didn't know how many other former *Mujahideen* of my acquaintance were still alive or if they were, then where they were living.

In Afghanistan or elsewhere.

This was something only my host would be able to tell me.

I almost backed out of the trip on more than one occasion as I was scared of what I may, or may not, find.

It was with nerves strung out at fever pitch that I finally left my mountain home for the long drive to the airport and the shorter flight to Kabul.

In a strange way…I was going home.

B.K. Zahrah Nasir
Bhurban
Pakistan

PART ONE

– I –

Climbing the morning mountain.

Slippery rocks.

Bird song echoing through remnants of pine forest.

Everything swirling silvery grey in the mist.

One hundred *kali kurta*, midnight blue with flowers and festive silver embroidery.

Snow white *chadar* ready to hide in.

Brown suede sandal shod feet labouring.

Brown leather shoulder bag bulging.

Embroidered cloth and leather backpack heavy with cameras, notebooks pens.

Apprehensively eager yet petrified.

A freezing numbness where my stomach is supposed to be.

A head full of convoluted memories all trying to rush into focus at once.

Eyes filled with images past and gone.

Proud faces, bandoliers of bullets, Kalashnikovs.

The reverberating sound of bombs...of planes...the chop, chop, chop of helicopter rotor blades closing in for the kill.

A hand raised in farewell.

Frightened of the path I have chosen to travel but no turning back, not now...just like the last time...the journey has begun.

– II –

A yellow cab from Bhurban to the airport not hearing a word the driver utters.

Hearing voices, accents and inflections from twenty-one years ago.

'Banafsha-Khomar. Banafsha-Khomar.'

'Ride like elastic.'

'*Sabaz chai* or *Tor chai.*'

'The Russians come. They bomb-bomb.'

Wondering if they would sound the same.

Wondering who was still there, alive...or dead on some unnamed battlefield.

Leaning towards learning with each winding bend of the torturously twisted road.

Yearning to know...yet not know the answers which have eluded me for so long.

Only one answer I know for definite.

Commander Anwar is still there.

In Afghanistan.

In Kabul.

In government now, not leading *Mujahideen* in Jegdalek.

Fighting a different fight in a different world and on a different basis but what of my hero, Commander Gul Ruz and what of '*The Gun Tree*' under which I sought refuge from a war which shattered my very core of being, then rebuilt my spirit in another mode?

Do I really want to go back?

– III –

The airport.

Hot, busy, heavily guarded, heavily stamped with finality as I handover my ticket, book in my small suitcase and take the few short steps to immigration.

Perhaps they will find something wrong with my passport, my visa, my person, but of course they won't, and don't.

The flight is far from full and two women immediately attract my attention.

Diplomats, journalists, aid workers?

Dust Motes – 1

Bundled up in a black *chadar*, round face, smiling, and uncovered, hands and feet intricately decorated with flowered scrolls of henna, Zohra sips her hot cup of tea with relish.

'I was born in Kabul,' she tells me sweeping the Executive Class Departure Lounge with almond shaped hazel eyes. 'We left there six months after the "Saur" Revolution in 1978 when I was a child and those six months were spent in Jail. Pul-e-Charki prison on the outskirts of the city.'

Thoughtfully nibbling a hard biscuit her face takes on a faraway look before she explains further, 'We were placed under house arrest within twenty-four hours of the revolution as my father was a religious leader and the new regime felt he could cause problems for them. At this point all the men of the family, my father and grandfather amongst them, were taken away to jail and the women and children were kept under guard in the house. We never saw the men again and eventually presumed that they had been executed. It was years later that this was confirmed in an article about my grandfather, written by a KGB guy, that someone saw and told us about. We still don't have the exact details about this or the fate of my father and I don't suppose we ever will. All we know is that they are dead. They were in the same jail as Hamid Karzai's uncle and when the guards came to take this man to be executed he put up a fierce fight. He had got hold of a knife from somewhere and stabbed at least one of his guards so they shot him on the spot. No. We are not related to the Karzais or to the Monarchy but we do have respect for them.'

In very precise, carefully worded English with a flat, international accent, Zohra told how she and other young girls of the immediate family were taken from the house to school and back each day with an armed escort but this didn't last long.

'The next thing we knew is that we too were in jail,' she continued grimacing at the memory. 'Then someone arranged something for us and after six months of incarceration we were suddenly put on a plane to India, at no notice and with absolutely no time to tell anyone where we were going to or to take anything with us other than the clothes we wore.'

I had already guessed that Zohra came from a wealthy background, to be 'rescued' in such a manner confirmed this assumption, as did the fact that she is obviously well educated and well travelled as visits to Spain, Italy, Bahrain and Britain had been mentioned, and even now, aged somewhere in her early thirties, I would say, she was travelling unescorted which is definitely not allowed in the case of Afghan women of a different class.

'From India we went to an aunt in Lahore, who I just visited on my way here,' she laughed, holding out her hands for inspection. 'The henna was in celebration of our reunion.' I didn't notice a wedding ring, wondered about this but decided against asking.

'Then from Lahore we went to an uncle in Germany as my mother needed treatment for cancer. For the first few years in Germany my mother kept saying, "We don't need to buy this and we don't need to buy that. There is no need to buy an apartment, we will just rent one as we will all be going home soon." But...after about five years we realized that this was not going to happen.'

Zohra first returned to Afghanistan, in the company of a cousin, in 2003 after an absence of twenty-three years and is now returning, alone, to stay with relatives outside Kabul, to spend six months leave from her job as a high ranking financial consultant in Germany, looking around to see what, if anything, she can do to help put her country back on its feet.

'I don't want to get involved in an NGO or something official,' she summed up. 'I just want to help in my own way as best as I can, in whatever field I can. It is, after all, my country and I am an Afghan.'

Fluent in Farsi, Pashto, Urdu, German and English, blessed with a lively, outgoing personality, with enough financial backing and plenty of excess baggage to boot, here is one young lady who not only knows her mind but, despite her privileged background still has a heart which is in the right place.

DUST MOTES – 2

Of medium height and extremely slight build, Fatima, with her incredibly dazzling, impish grin, would stand out in any crowd and in the almost empty lounge she made quite an impact. It is almost impossible not to stare at her but I imagine that she is quite used to this.

The saying 'black is beautiful' is particularly applicable in her case.

'Me?' she drawls in an obvious American accent whilst pointing a long, delicate, heavily be-ringed index finger at her own chest.

'Why do you want to know about me?' Before I can answer she tells me anyway.

'Well. Briefly. I was born and brought up in Eritrea but got the opportunity to relocate to America where I went to school, college and Uni. Hey! I am one lucky girl!' She laughs gaily whilst performing arabesques with her finely formed hands. The young man behind the refreshment counter almost passes out at the stunning sight of this ebony black, fantasy creature, sitting in his lounge, in his patch, wearing a high fashion *shalwar kameez* consisting of very fine, almost transparent embroidered cotton, the bell-bottom *shalwar* slit almost to the knee, the short, tight, apology for a *kameez* slit from bangle adorned, bone-thin wrist to model elbow.

'I just love to travel the big wide world and while I'm doing this I just love to buy jewellery, jewellery and more jewellery. Not the expensive stuff. Not like gold.' She rolls the word 'gold' around the back of her throat much as she comically rolls her enormous eyes towards the grubby ceiling and then in the direction of her over-bulging backpack, handbag and an enormous carrier bag bearing the slogan of a boutique in Lahore. 'I really should have sent some of this stuff home by DHL before travelling on you know. I don't suppose I can do that in Kabul can I? Better do it when I go back to India. I just can't resist jewellery, particularly all the gorgeous silver stuff you have here. The big chunky stuff you know. Just look at what I got in my bag.'

Both Zohra and I advise her not to spread her precious jewellery out all over the lounge for hungry eyes to see. Not everyone considers silver jewellery to be cheap and who knows where word spreads. Fatima was just too open for her own good.

'Then there's fabric you know. You have such wonderful fabrics, here and in India. I've already shipped tons of fabric back home which I will have made up into things, you know "things", when I get back. Whenever I go travelling I always but always have to ship things home and still have to pay an exorbitant amount in excess baggage. Can you believe that?'

We can indeed!

'Hey.' She waves to the enraptured attendant. 'Do you think we can have some more tea and cookies over here?' He can't believe his luck and almost falls flat on his feet as he rushes to meet her wish.

'I'm kind of on a one year's travel. Sri Lanka, India, Vietnam, Malaysia, Singapore, Pakistan. Now some NGO has offered me a job in Afghanistan so, as I'm in the locality, I thought I'd better check it out before signing anything. You see I know absolutely zilch about the conditions there or the customs so just decided to drop by and take a look.'

This woman, again I would think to be in her early thirties, has absolutely no idea what she is doing or what she is getting herself into.

'Obviously I know there was a war there and that stuff is in kind of a mess right now. In flux if you like. That's why I'm checking it out first. After all, if you were born in Eritrea then you gotta know something about war and what happens to ordinary people. I was real lucky you know. Not like some.'

'Are they expecting you?' queried a concerned Zohra.

'No. Not at all. Just thought I'd drop by and see. I'll phone them once I get to a hotel.' Fatima replied with a dismissive gesture.

'Have you booked a hotel?' I asked this self-destructive creature.

'No. I'll take a cab from the airport and ask the driver where to go.'

Innocence abroad. Overconfident innocence at that!

The financial consultant in Zohra came to the fore. 'Have you changed your money to Afghanis?' she politely enquired.

'Gee. I didn't think of that,' replied a wide-eyed Fatima. 'I guess there will be an ATM and I have my credit card.'

We both shook our heads in disbelief.

Who on earth was this naive person? Did she think she was merely on one more tourist jaunt?

Kabul is not exactly the safest place on earth right now and won't be for a long, long time to come.

'You can't take a cab,' Zohra insisted. 'It's not a safe thing to do. I'm being met by relatives at the airport and we pass close by the Continental Hotel on our way home. We'll give you a lift. It would be better this way.'

'Oh wow! That would be just great,' Fatima gushed. 'I really don't know anything about the place you see.'

I dug in my own bag and handed her my precious copy of a recently published *Guide to Kabul* advising her to read it on the plane but to please give it back once we landed in Kabul.

This was my first visit to the city too.

'Hey. If I wear one of my *saris* I guess they'll take me for an Indian,' she confided before heading off to tidy up in the ladies room when the flight was called.

Fatima claimed to be a social worker, working for a few months in America, taking a year off to travel, then walking into another lucrative job on her return and repeating the process. I honestly wondered about this. If she really is a social worker then who looks after her?

– IV –

'Are you being met at the airport Banafsha?' Zohra asked.

'Were you born in Kabul or are you from another part of the country?'

'Yes. I'm being met but no, I'm not from Afghanistan,' I replied to her surprise.

I didn't try to explain.

How could I?

When I first went to Afghanistan I went as one person.

When I left…it was as someone else.

This 'me'…the person who exists now…emerged from the war-shattered womb of Afghanistan.

Clawed her way into this reality out of an emotional morass of bewilderment.

Out of fear.

Out of pain.

Out of death and confusion.

Commander Anwar's mother in a tented Peshawar refugee camp held out her arms.

'You cannot be alone. This is wrong. So now you are my daughter, I am your mother and we are your family. Stay with us. You have come home.'

How I longed to remain.

Oh how I was drawn to remain but didn't...couldn't if I was to keep my promise of telling the world what was happening in Afghanistan under Soviet occupation.

I hadn't yet learnt that the world wasn't interested.

That blow came later.

In Scotland.

When I learnt the hard way.

Totally obsessed with my mission.

Totally demoralized by the result.

No one wanted to know.

The truth was a bitter pill to swallow.

I saw my Afghan mother once more.

A tall house behind a guarded compound wall.

Kalashnikovs at the ready.

Still in Peshawar then.

Eight years later.

Surrounded by my 'sisters' who piled my arms with my *Jahez*.

'This is not our tradition,' she told me, the years showing in her lined and saddened face.

'But you married a Pakistani and the tradition is theirs.'

'This is the first time we have seen you since your *shadi* and you cannot leave from your father's house empty-handed.'

A hand-embroidered *chadar* that I wear with pride.

An embroidered *shalwar kameez*.

A handful of shimmering uncut stones, here a ruby, there an emerald, a topaz, a piece of lapis lazuli the blue stone of Afghanistan found nowhere else in the world.

The gift of acceptance, of a belonging that I never felt before.

Adopted for the second time.

A homecoming of a very special sort.

Commander Anwar was there too.

Lounging against a green velvet cushion, a glass of black tea by his side.

Khaki *shalwar kameez* like before.

Radiating charisma.

Exactly like before.

Cracking walnuts and *kagazi badam* in powerful hands.

Cracking a smile and an inquisition.

Bodyguards outside.

His own captured Russian pistol in its worn leather holster.

Flap fastened tight.

For now.

'We leave for Afghanistan in the morning,' he said, rolling his English around the back of his throat, expelling it with a whistle through a small gap in his teeth.

'This time we will win.' A statement of fact.

'You will come with us again Banafsha. You will witness our triumph. We leave at dawn.'

'I can't,' I whispered, wishing it was otherwise.

'I must return to my husband in Karachi. He will not give his permission.'

'You didn't need permission before,' he retorted, throwing in a mischievous smile to break the edge.

'I wasn't married then,' flashed back like semaphore.

His eyes bored into mine. 'I know,' he said with a teasing look of remembrance. 'I know.'

The family was in mourning.

Arif, a younger brother had been murdered.

A dark night in Peshawar.

An argument.

A knife.

Another life gone.

I remember his smile.

Mischievous, full of morning sunlight and brave expectations against the odds.

His new wife.

Tribal facial tattoos, flower shadows in the light of a hissing kerosene lamp, shyly peeking at me in a mosquito buzzing, biting night of the time before.

A widow now.

Dark and sombre, sobbing in a corner with a child in her arms.

Broken.

Only three weeks since her life was shattered.

What was her future now?

We ate.

We talked.

We dozed awhile and then I left.

A family *shadi*, my husband's Pathan relatives.

Commander Anwar came that evening bringing Gulshan, his sister, my sister Laila's daughter with him.

Bodyguards hovering discretely.

A waif escaping from mourning into the joys that she found.

Sitting on the bride's lap tracing hennaed patterns, playing with her necklace, trying on her *churis*, trying on happiness for size.

Finding that it fit.

'How is Gul Ruz?' I asked Commander Anwar in trepidation, the letters, images, the ruby he gave me, the unwritten promise that I hadn't kept. 'How is he?'

'He's fine.'

I waited for more.

There wasn't any.

I no longer had the right to ask.

'We leave at dawn.'

The words flung over his shoulder into the *motia* perfumed night.

'It is right that you should be with us.'

I followed his retreating back with my Afghan mind.

Gulshan skipped beside him until they were swallowed in the gloom.

A flight to Karachi next morning.

Searching the high mountain passes with eyes that no one else should ever see.

Picturing the *Mujahideen* walking towards their destiny.

Wanting to be there too.

Wondering where it would end...for all of us.

Dinner in Karachi.

A formal affair.

Benazir Bhutto the guest of honour.

No honour in me being there and feeling it.

Social chit chat.

'Do you know the name of the style of embroidery on Benazir's *kameez*?' a voice dripping gold, diamonds and milk fed mangoes enquired.

'Of course,' I replied into a sudden hush in the women filled space. 'Benazir is wearing *Zardari* work.'

Gasps of shock, horror.

A mistake that I didn't care to rectify.

'We leave at dawn,' was the only voice in my head.

– V –

More passengers arrive at the last minute.

Returning Afghans.

Women in Iranian style coats and headscarves.

Husband, wife, three children.

She in an old-fashioned, wool, black trouser suit, startling white joggers.

He, 1950s Mafioso style double-breasted, shiny suit.

Their children in bright shorts and T-shirts.

Candy pink, brilliant turquoise, Mickey Mouse motifs.

A few Pakistani businessmen on the make.

More Europeans than I've seen at one time for years.

Investors, Social Workers, Journalists?

A tremendously obese, fair, sharp-nosed 'wifey' with 'Made in the United States of America Missionary' stamped all over her long black skirt and white blouse.

Hardly time to sneeze before we land in Peshawar.

'For refuelling,' says the announcer's voice.

I wonder why...we've only just left Islamabad. It doesn't make sense.

Numerous passengers stridently objecting to the stop-over.

Didn't they read the schedule?

Some idiots insisting that they are disembarking to walk around, stretch their legs, phone relatives.

Machine-guns, ready and pointing, mounted on the back of pick-up trunks don't look very inviting.

I would freak out if I wasn't accustomed to such things.

So many passengers queuing up to board that I wonder if they will fit.

A totally different category of people than those already seated.

Wild men.

Gulbuddin Hekmatyar look-alikes returning from the Gulf.

Sunshine yellow Kuwait Duty Free carrier bags bulging with loot.

Hands reaching up to adjust air vents.

A forest of hairy limbs sporting the biggest gold watches ever.

They must be fake...or...maybe not...the Customs guys will know.

Airborne.

Butterflies in my head now as well as in my stomach.

Butterflies in my arms and legs.

Mountains in my eyes.

This must be one of the most spectacular flights on earth.

The lush green agricultural holdings of Pakistan changing to mountains, mountains and more mountains with harsh desert valleys trapped in-between.

Peaks with snow, sifted icing sugar, delicate scrolls, needle-like pinnacles of naked rock spearing drifts of sun reflecting clouds.

Did I really travel through this terrain on foot, on horseback, in a war?

Did I pass through that valley or this one?

Jegdalek is down there somewhere.

So is Tora Ara.

A mountainside dressed in lavender.

A song on the perfumed breeze.

Gul Ruz on a horse.

Bandoliers of bullets.

Kalashnikov used to indicate directions.

Jalalabad, Sarobi, Zazi, Pakistan, Russia.

Now Kabul.

Smaller than I imagined.

The ghetto-like concrete blocks of Microrayon apartments dominating a dust bowl set in mountains.

A city struggling to rise from its own ashes.

Coming up quickly.

Coming in to land.

DUST MOTES – 3

'I will meet you myself. You will be my guest and I will be completely at your disposal whilst you are in Kabul,' stressed Sayed Mahmood Zia Dashti when I'd spoken to him by phone a few days previously.

'I will drive you around. Show you the sights. Escort you to a *kurash* match. You can photograph the wrestlers and interview them if you like,' he gushed, bonhomie almost making him stutter at the prospect. His voice a high nasal twang, the type of tone often associated with someone suffering from a hearing defect. Accent, mid-European.

Mr Jekdalek is in the Gulf on business but he will return before you arrive in Kabul. His mother and family are here also. I will personally telephone him right now and inform him of your schedule. Did you have any problems getting your visa?'

'No. No problem at all.'

Stretching a point as I had faced a problem.

Filling in the form at the tiny, security glassed visa application window hidden round the back of the Afghan Embassy in Islamabad while the two men on duty stared at me in a puzzled manner.

Pushing the completed form with its two required passport-sized photographs beneath the grill only to have everything immediately pushed back and a disembodied voice ask, 'Why are you applying for a visa? You should get your passport renewed instead and then you can come and go as you please.'

Passport. What passport?

'I am happy to see that you are going home. We need educated people to return and help in the reconstruction. Are you a teacher?'

'I've never had an Afghan passport,' I informed the well-meaning moustached, balding man behind the dirty glass.

'Born in one of the refugee camps were you? Well just bring the papers from there or bring your parents' papers and we will issue you with a passport in no time at all.'

Nice offer...no dice.

None of Dashti's affair.

I had met this earnest young man about six weeks prior to my trip.

A member of the 'New Afghanistan'.

A different 'tribe' than those rugged mountain *Mujahideen* I had come to know and respect.

A highly educated, citified Afghan.

A suit and tie, impeccably starched and pressed Afghan, completely at ease in the lobby of the Marriot Hotel in Islamabad.

As vice president of the Afghan National Olympic Committee he was accompanying a large number of athletes, male, and surprisingly enough, female, who were competing in the Asian Games in the run up to the Athens Olympics.

I had been trying, in vain, to get Commander Anwar's Kabul telephone number for the last couple of years.

Ever since I learnt that he was first the 'Mayor of Kabul' and then 'President of the Afghan National Olympic Committee'.

The embassy in Islamabad couldn't help.

Mr Assadullah Tarzi, Second Secretary, tried his best but telephone connections in Kabul are rare, mobiles predominate and individual's numbers, particularly of those in positions of power, almost State secrets.

He did though manage to put me in touch with Dashti who possessed not one but two mobile telephone numbers for his exalted 'Mr Jekdalek'.

The 'Mr Jekdalek' was a new one to me.

It had always been either 'Commander Anwar' or, more simply, 'Anwar'.

The majority of Afghans do not posses a second name.

I presume he decided to add the 'Jekdalek', when his star began to ascend on the new political horizon.

This addition also served to inform those who didn't already know that he was, and is, the renowned 'Commander Anwar' who led his *Mujahideen* on the 'Jegdalek Front' in their ferocious fight against the Russian invaders.

Not a man to be treated lightly.

Dashti, also president of the Afghan Kurash Federation, had a little difficulty in understanding that I had travelled to Jegdalek with his hero.

'You were there!!! ??? During the war?' eyebrows raised so high as to converge with his hairline. Mouth gaping, startled eyes wide open, ears actually twitching and hands clasping and unclasping themselves as he bounced up and down on the edge of his seat. 'You were really there?'

An archetypal 'Boys Own' character come to life.

Too young to have participated himself, though, not really to be honest.

Whilst he laboured over school, college, university books in some unnamed foreign country, boys, mere children far younger than he, carried whatever weapons they could get their hands on, guns, catapults, stones, soft drink bottles full of petrol with a rag for a fuse, others were completely empty-handed but they fought…and died for their homes, villages, towns, cities, for honour and for Afghanistan.

The difference between the haves and the have-nots of the world we live in.

Their reward…nothing if they managed to survive…the label 'martyr' if they didn't.

Dashti, of two constantly ringing mobile phones and plugged in laptop computer came out ahead.

'I have just learnt, a couple of hours ago in fact,' he informed me in a voice so full of pride that he could only control it with great difficulty but, even so, it managed to race up and down the scales at a speed so rapid as to be almost unintelligible. 'Mr Jekdalek has been appointed as "Special Advisor" to President Hamid Karzai. This is a great honour for him and for all of us.'

'Special Advisor in what field?' I asked.

His eyebrows performed somersaults. How dare I even ask!

He didn't, or couldn't explain further.

This was more than enough for him.

Riding so closely in the wake of power obviously gave him an incredible 'high'.

Maybe some of the glitz, glitter and, inevitably money, would rub off on him.

At least he would be a familiar, English speaking face, to greet me on my arrival.

– VI –

Landed with a whump on the patched and weedy runway.

Eyes curiously searching the surroundings for the fabled 'airplane graveyard' much touted in the press.

I couldn't see it anywhere.

Maybe they cleaned it up.

What I did see gave me goosebumps.

Members of the so-called International Security Assistance Force.

Strutting their stuff.

Menacing everyone in sight.

Sheer brutality in desert combat gear.

All cast in Arnold Schwarzenegger mode.

All with boots and guns at the ready.

All leering at every female around.

It felt as if I was entering a high security jail not a 'free country'.

Not a 'liberated zone'.

Certainly not the Afghanistan of memory.

Afghan airport police in total contrast.

Polite, smiling, respectful.

Through immigration at the speed of light.

Ladies first here.

No shoving and pushing.

Ladies first.

Reassuring.

My new white *chadar* firmly in place.

Hiding now.

Trying to become anonymous.

Trying not to be scared.

DUST MOTES – 4

A heavily muscled young man, blue jeans, black T-shirt waving a 'Miss Banafsha' sign.

A highly excited, beaming older man dancing on the spot next to him.

Grey beard, grey hair, white teeth flashing a million dollar smile.

Barrel-chest bursting with pride.

Drab green *shalwar kameez*, black waistcoat, crisp and smart.

Black boots, mirror finished.

'Banafsha-Khomar. Banafsha-Khomar,' he was yelling at the top of his voice.

'Welcome. Welcome to Kabul. Welcome home.'

If I had been male he would have swept me off my feet in a bear hug.

His joy was infectious.

Suddenly everyone was smiling.

Police.

Security guards.

Males and females but not the foreign soldiers who stared at the evolving scene with intense dislike, disquiet…it was hard to be sure of any emotion emanating from them except animosity.

'Hi there!' said the muscular young man with a New York twang. 'I'm Mr Jekdalek's assistant. He sent me to meet you and Commander Telabaz insisted on coming along too as he said that he would recognize you from before.'

Commander Telabaz, grinning like an idiot, one arm flung around the burly shoulders of an airport security guard, waiting for me to connect.

I smiled back.

The name was not familiar but there was something in the face that was.

The seconds ticked by…time stretched.

His utter delight began to be replaced by a creeping disappointment.

I wracked my memory.

1,500 *Mujahideen* in long ago Jegdalek.

Which one was this?

Who was he?

As the muscle bursting T-shirt yanked my luggage off the squeaking carousel asking 'Is this all? Just one piece?' It hit me.

It couldn't be but it was.

It was Jonsey!

I'd never known his name so gave him one of my own as he reminded me of a kid on the British Council estate of my childhood.

Jonsey!

He certainly hadn't been a Commander then.

'Tora Ara?' I said.

A query to which he laughed out loud in pleasure whilst simultaneously thumping the unsuspecting security guard so hard on the chest that he sat down, hard, amongst the still moving luggage, managing to loosen his lethal looking pistol from its unfastened halter in the process.

'Tora Ara,' he happily agreed then loosed a torrent of 'Dari' which lost me completely.

Yes.

I knew him now.

That magical day of butterflies, ricocheting bullets, distant bombs and always the fragrance of lavender.

'One in front, one behind, side by side we rode down a dried up riverbed, of blood and stones.'

Commander Gul Ruz and I.

Jonsey on foot.

Young then.

A black stubble of beard on his chin.

Bare feet in shabby sandals.

Not even a gun to call his own.

Arms full of anti-tank missiles when we returned to Jegdalek base camp in the evening.

Eyes full of dreams, heroes and martyrs.

So.

He is here.

He has survived.

He even has a Toyota Corolla which he drives with a nonchalance that was not evident before.

Security passes on the front and rear windshields.

Even a pass for the high security, off-limits to all, Presidential Palace.

He has come up from the ranks.

Jonsey has done well.

– VII –

Fatima had disappeared, taking my precious guidebook with her.

Asked 'T-shirt' if he'd seen her.

'A black lady? Yes. Gone to the VIP lounge.'

So we went there and found her arm in arm with Zohra who is, as I thought, someone of importance but whom?

A whole fleet of shiny Pajeros, extra-dark tinted windows, bristling with guards and guns was waiting to take her 'home'. Take her back to jail?

House arrest?

Definitely escort her somewhere.

She suddenly looked drawn and tense.

She certainly wasn't smiling now.

She didn't speak to me either just pulled her black *chadar* closer.

A crow?

A crone?

I could have been invisible.

'If I'd known some of the stuff in this book then I sure would have stayed in India,' gasped a very flustered Fatima as she handed it over.

'It's pretty scary huh?' her eyes wide open now.

'All that stuff about personal security wow! And the mines! I don't think I'll be here for long and I don't think I'll be staying anyplace except inside the hotel. It's just...like...wow!!!!' Huge round eyes echoing her shocked 'O' of a pink tinted mouth.

Pulling her white lacey headscarf a little tighter, exposing most of her velvet black arms in the process and managing to attract even more attention than ever, she strode quickly to the nearest Pajero and hopped inside.

Maybe she was under arrest too!

I'd found some of the information rather worrying also but...no turning back now.

Feet on the ground and forwards!

The fleet of ominous looking vehicles spun up a cloud of dust peppered with small stones as it raced from sight.

It rounded a corner and was gone.

'Who was that?' asked 'T-shirt' as Commander Telabaz patted grit out of his waistcoat, scowling ferociously at the imagined insult.

'I really don't know,' I answered. 'Just someone I met at the airport.'

– VIII –

The road from the airport was wide. In good repair and lined with undamaged houses.

Not what I expected at all.

The traffic seemed more 'sane' than at home in Pakistan.

The trucks, disappointingly, undecorated.

Bland and dusty.

I wondered if Pakistani trucks went through a paint job at the border!

They brought me here.

A small 'villa' with a large over-grown lawn only a five minute drive from the airport and where Laila's son, Farhad, lives.

DUST MOTES – 5

'Hi! Banafsha,' said the tall, rather lanky, figure in jeans and T-shirt towering over me and holding out a bony hand to shake.

I searched for clues but didn't find any.

He reminded me of Lawrence.

The son of a friend from way back in another time, another place.

He could have been his twin.

'I'm Laila's son, Farhad.' He informed me with a slight, nervous stutter in a distinctly London voice, finger brushing wind-blown hair out of his eyes whilst attempting a hesitant smile.

'You were just a little boy in the refugee camp in Peshawar,' I gasped in astonishment, memory performing cartwheels. 'Weren't you the one who got bitten by a scorpion?'

His turn to be surprised.

'Yeah. That was me. You remember that!'

'You screamed blue murder. People were suddenly running in all directions at once and I didn't know what was going on.'

A humid Peshawar night in August.

The tented camp, sweating humanity, and mosquitoes.

The hiss of kerosene lamps.

Soft dying thuds of suicidal moths.

Women chattering and giggling behind their hands.

A bottle of Pepsi that I didn't want.

Relaxing.

Then a high, shrill scream tore the night apart.

Chaos.

A grey-bearded elder.

Anwar's father, my father, holding a huge, glinting knife into the flickering flame of a smoky candle, turning it blue.

His other arm encompassing a wildly struggling child.

His mouth voicing endearments.

The knife flashing.

The child screaming again.

The mouth now sucking on tender flesh.

Spitting blood.

Sucking and spitting.

The child crying.

The women showing me the squashed scorpion.

Myself suddenly afraid of the dark.

How could I forget?

'Hey...Banafsha remembers that bloody scorpion! Damned thing hurt like hell,' he told Commander Telabaz, T-shirt and the armed guards who had rushed out of the guardhouse to greet me. 'Wait until I tell Mum. By the way, she phoned earlier, from London, and I told her you were arriving. She called you by another name. Pam. Yes. That was it, Pam.'

It was originally Pam at the point of first meeting.

Maria before that...but that's yet another story.

Changed to Banafsha-Khomar in Afghanistan where I was named after a well known singer.

A sinus problem in the night.

I snored.

'Aah! She sings!!!' was the amused observation and an embarrassed Banafsha-Khomar entered the world.

Changed to Zahrah when I emigrated to Pakistan and now, back in Afghanistan the *Khomar* has been dropped as it really isn't very flattering, now I'm Banafsha. Just Banafsha.

I had been under the impression that I would be staying with Anwar's mother, my mother.

'She left. Went back to London a while ago,' Farhad told me. 'So Anwar thought it best that you stay here. He's just coming. He should be here any minute now.'

I am unaccountably nervous.

'Anyway. Come in. I'll show you your room and you can have tea. You probably need it after your trip.'

My room.

A beautiful, large, hand woven carpet on the floor.

A 'Shirazi'.

Once predominantly red and blue, the red now faded to rose.

I wonder how it managed to survive the wars, the revolutions, the looters and the Taliban.

The walls lined with seven mattresses and seven pillows, all covered in matching nylon velvet printed with black, imitation 'Elephant's Foot' on a deep crimson background.

Acrylic curtains billow inwards, blown by the increasingly strong, increasingly dusty wind.

They are faded cream with green tulips sprouting out of a fountain.

There are lots of large, open windows, some with jali.

Grossly ornate light fittings.

No punkha.

The ceiling is low.

The room is incredibly hot.

'I hope you will be comfortable in here,' says Farhad as Commander Telabaz plonks himself down on one of the mattresses, coughing as a cloud of dust rises to envelope him.

'If you need a bed then I'll see if I can find one.'

'No. It's okay. I can manage,' I tell him.

'Of course Banafsha. You travelled with Mujahideen so you are used to sleeping in more uncomfortable places than this.' He states with a still shy grin.

'Let me introduce you to Naeem. He looks after the house during the day and will be around to bring food, tea or whatever you need.'

'Naeem,' he bellows in the direction of the minute kitchen where the kettle is already coming to the boil.

'He speaks some Urdu so you won't have any problem in communicating with him,' Farhad adds as the ferocious visage of a fully fledged bandit appears around the open door.

Dust Motes – 6

Naeem, a Shia Hazara from the persecuted Bamiyan region of Central Afghanistan.

A direct descendant of the 'Hordes of Genghis Khan'.

Highly prominent slanting cheekbones, tip-tilted eyes shielded by folds of yellowish skin, a Mongol to the core.

The majority of Hazaras in Kabul are limited to menial work and are often despised, certainly distrusted.

If they have found employment in a household then, come sunset, they must leave.

Head back to their shanty villages on the outskirts of the city.

Head home to find the strength to live another day.

They are, quite openly and obviously, just as downtrodden as ever.

Naeem serves green tea, politely avoiding looking in my direction.

Commander Telabaz demands sweets to celebrate my arrival.

He speaks fluent Urdu now and expects me to understand.

I gather that his family is still in Haripur, NWFP, Pakistan.

Children at school and college and he doesn't want to disrupt their education at such a crucial juncture.

He recalls visits to Murree and Nathia Gali with nostalgia and is still trying to figure out where Bhurban is, as for some unknown reason he thought I lived in Kashmir, when we are interrupted.

Farhad's mobile phone rings shrilly, demanding immediate attention.

'*Balay*,' he answers as he rushes out into the garden where reception is clearer, then races back in, issues instructions to Commander

Telabaz who, reluctantly struggles to his feet, tells me 'That was Anwar. We have to go to a meeting. Sorry about this Banafsha. Anwar will come later.'

Then they are gone.

I'm still waiting.

How well I remember all the waiting for something to happen.

The only difference now is that I am sitting on a mattress not leaning on 'The Gun Tree'.

The compound is surrounded by high concrete walls.

The armed guards reside in a long, low building which takes up all of the front wall except for a bright blue, iron gate.

The guards are screened off from me by a hastily constructed 'purdah curtain', consisting of a wooden frame onto which a wide length of canvas has been nailed. A second length of canvas, this one suspended from a rope, hangs across the driveway.

I can't see the guards, only their feet as they wander around.

I can't see the outside world either.

I hear traffic zooming past, horns blowing.

I see the rims of bicycle wheels from under the front gate.

I also see the feet of passing men and the fast swirling hems of blue burkhas.

I am suspended in the atmosphere.

Drifting in time.

Waiting.

– IX –

Naeem brought a fresh pot of green tea before leaving for the night.

Warned me against drinking the water.

Warned me to always keep my suitcase packed and locked.

The door too.

Then disappeared in a mad swirl of wind-blown dust, black and white chequered *chadar* clamped between gleaming teeth, huge *kukri* firmly in his belt, leaving me wondering what the bodyguards were for.

Weren't they here for my security?

Were bandits going to scale the walls?

Taliban mount a fully fledged assault?

What kind of place was I staying in?

More to the point…was I safe here?

Trying to keep myself awake I decided it best to familiarize myself with the villa.

Where was the back door for example?

Directly across the spacious hallway from my room was the room which Farhad used in the daytime.

It was a mirror of my own with the addition of a single bed, a huge television, video and music system.

An enlarged colour photograph of Anwar and Ahmed Shah Massoud in a bear hug on one wall.

Smaller framed photographs.

A picture gallery.

The glory days mounted on the cracked cement wall of a Russian built 'home' which didn't feel like anyone's home at all.

A passing through place.

Lifeless.

Somehow soulless and forlorn.

Two back rooms, one of them Farhad's private quarters, both firmly padlocked.

A reasonable sized bathroom, not very clean and housing two loos, one a squat, the other normal, a grubby bathtub, a broken shower, and surprisingly enough, a washing machine. Made in Gujranwalla, a twin to the one I have at home.

The kitchen, minuscule.

Nothing more than a walk-in-cupboard with a two ring gas stove and cylinder on the grimy floor.

Unwashed dishes in the sink.

Cracked crockery and mismatched cutlery on a couple of greasy shelves and two stubs of Chinese made candles.

No fridge.

Nothing to drink except tea.

Absolutely nothing to eat and I'm hungry.

More importantly…no back door.

No way out except the front and no safe place to hide if there is an attack.

There could be.

This is still a city under siege in many respects.

Foreign troops, hiding inside armoured personnel carriers, in convoys for safety, patrol the streets.

Thunder past the blue gate.

Make the window frames rattle and put my blood pressure up.

The wind throws empty cans of 'Valkyrie' beer clattering around in the narrow alley on the kitchen side of the house and my nerves correspond.

A battered cardboard carton of stale *nan* skips sideways across the 'lawn'.

I think that there may be a vehicle arriving.

Yes.

Car tyres at the gate.

Feet…but not Anwar.

A change of bodyguard.

I feel as if I'm under house arrest.

Solitary confinement.

Farhad said to help myself to his TV but I didn't come to Kabul to watch Indian movies.

This is boring!

Two hours later and the room is finally cooling down.

Feel like sleeping, food, drink or not.

If I do then either Anwar or Farhad are sure to arrive.

I wonder if the traffic outside these walls ever stops, or the planes or helicopters overhead?

Actually, I'm too tired to care.

Another hour.

I shouldn't have come.

Farhad arrived back in a rush clutching a 'Hang Ten' bag.

'Anwar brought me something from Kuwait when he was there last week,' he says rushing off into his room to change his clothes whilst shouting back over his shoulder, 'He has been invited out. I have to go with him. He'll come in the morning around 10 o'clock. Sorry about this. You know how it is.'

I don't but keep quiet.

Emerging in a freshly pressed *shalwar kameez*, cursing the dust on his shoes, wiping them on the nearest curtain, he continues, 'I've ordered food and water for you. You're quite safe here but leave all the lights on. The guard is just outside. Call him if you need anything.' Then he's gone, a shadow into the threatening night.

I should have remembered that sometimes it's better not to 'go back'.

Keep the memories.

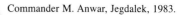
Commander M. Anwar, Jegdalek, 1983.

Mohammad Anwar Jekdalek, 2004.

Commander Gul Ruz, Tora Ara, 1983.

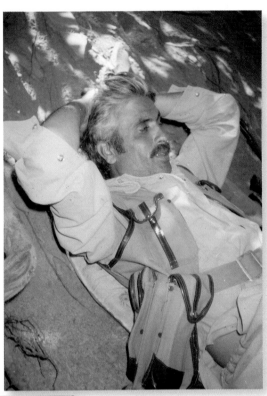

Commander Gul Ruz, 2004.

Rubina Mqueir.

Friba Rezzai.

Darwish.

Farhad.

America meets Kabul.

An incredible swimming pool.

Reservoir, Bagh-e-Babur.

Babur's tomb.

The Mausoleum of King Nadir Shah.

Shipping container stores.

Darulaman Palace.

Kargha Lake.

Take them out and look at them but don't, under any circumstances, go back.

Now disappointment looms.

Disillusionment takes hold.

I know that Anwar is a busy, important person, dashing around in his 'Gucci' shoes and expensive, western designer gear but...this is awful.

What has happened to traditional hospitality or just plain good manners?

A timid tap on the door.

The bodyguard, Kalashnikov over his shoulder, bandolier of bullets across his chest, has brought my supper.

At least he resembles the *Mujahideen* of memory although he's far too young to have been in Jegdalek.

'My elder brother was there at the same time as you,' he tells me.

'You must remember him. Half of his face was blown away.'

I can't bring anyone of this description to mind but smile and nod anyway.

He carefully spreads a small plastic tablecloth on the carpet, red and blue flowers adorned with spatters of dried up grease.

Stone cold mutton *kebab*, tepid *nan* and a carton of Pakistani yoghurt.

A box of tissues, also Pakistani.

Probably the meat and the flour for the *nan* are Pakistani too.

I've seen sacks of flour, donations to Afghanistan, in my local bazaar and once, years ago, cans of cooking oil in Karachi bearing the legend 'Gift of the Italian Government to the People of Afghanistan'. So anything is possible.

The mineral water is American.

The Pepsi I gave back to him.

I don't understand why they drink the stuff but maybe they don't know that a percentage of the purchase price goes back into the American arsenal to pay for the bombs and bullets which still rain down on Afghanistan at regular intervals.

I don't think they would contribute to the maiming of their own people, the laying to waste of their own country if they knew this.

Or, at least I hope not.

Kabul had such a 'small town' feel...initially but, suddenly it's too big and far too western for me.

Too 'American satellite' for my epicurean intellectual taste buds.

I must stop this.

I'm exhausted and jumping to conclusions which only time will confirm, not tiredness.

– X –

Huddled underneath a heavy red, black flowered blanket on a mattress.

Pillow over my ears to blot out the sound of shooting.

The dust laden wind shrieking at humanity.

Shrieking with humanity.

Carrying the voices of the dead.

The dispossessed.

The dispersed.

Wishing I was back in Jegdalek on my roof top *charpoy* surrounded by *Mujahideen* and a danger that was tangible.

Alone in my room, listening to the night sounds of Kabul, I am frightened.

Alien.

Heard Farhad creeping back in the early hours of the morning.

Imagined a thief, a rapist, a murderer.

Heard the bodyguard and knew it was alright.

Felt the sun come up, the wind die down and lay watching a multitude of spangled dust motes caught, imprisoned in a weak ray of sunlight.

Dawn.

A new day.

A day full to bursting with anticipation but no bird song.

No dawn chorus.

Not even the 'cawing' of a crow.

Wars do such things to cities.

Annihilate everything in their path.

Wipe the slate but certainly not clean.

Wars leave an agonized smear of molecules, human, animal, bird, plant bits all mashed together, struggling to breathe in a vast lake of slimy soup from which, if they are strong enough, some bits will emerge, reform and eventually repopulate.

END OF PART ONE

PART TWO

– I –

6 a.m. and a cold wash as I can't figure out the hot water system.

No signs of life inside the house but can hear plenty from outside, including the annoying, wheezing rattle of what may be a water pump next door.

Desperate for coffee but can't get the *chula* to work.

Drank water and ate the rest of last night's yoghurt.

Lost myself in memories and apprehension until 9 a.m. when Naeem's feet appeared underneath the *purdah* screen.

The dust-laden wind battered the front door *jali* back and fro as he entered, unlit cigarette dangling rakishly from the side of his unsmiling mouth.

Black and white chequered scarf firmly in place.

Tattered plastic shoes discarded on the door mat.

He looks just as sinister as ever.

The squeal of the door hinges, the clattering, sets my teeth on edge.

He silently, without being asked, put on the kettle and before he could make tea I requested plain boiling water so that I could finally make coffee.

Thank goodness I brought a jar with me!

Farhad has just surfaced looking bleary and...hung-over?

He mumbled something like 'Did I want bread with my tea?' whilst picking up a piece of yesterday's hard as a board *nan* off the dirty kitchen window sill, covered in a heaving mass of flies.

'No thanks,' I told him with a definite shake of my head.

'Shall I send out for cake?'

'No thanks. I had yoghurt.'

Groggily Farhad crawled back into his room.

Back to sleep I imagined, but just as I took the first sip of scalding coffee, he emerged, almost at a run, eyes struggling to focus.

'Thought I better phone Anwar and see what is happening,' he said. 'But I got Commander Telabaz who is in a car following three other cars. Anwar is in one of them but Telabaz doesn't know where they are going except that there was a call from some Minister or other.'

All the fun of the fair!

Obviously Anwar is not going to be here at 10 a.m.

Am I relieved or disappointed?

What do I do now?

DUST MOTES – 5

'Hey! Is that coffee? Real coffee,' asks Farhad with a glimmer of disbelief in his eyes and saliva at the corner of his twitching mouth.

'Want some?'

'Too right,' he replies, reaching for the jar, calling to Naeem for another cup and more hot water.

'I used to drink coffee all the time but since coming here I've stuck to bottled water mainly.'

I picture the empty beer cans out in the alley and smile.

'I've seen coffee in the bazaar, but well, you know, you can't be sure if it's the real thing or not so I haven't bought any.'

Thankfully he doesn't question the provenance of my Pakistani coffee as I sometimes have doubts about this too.

'There is this real cool coffee bar on King's Road. I used to love going there. Real cool. You must know the place.'

I don't but keep quiet and listen.

'We went to live in London, from Peshawar, on 10 October 1992. I remember the date exactly,' he beams with pride spooning a second helping of sugar into his brimming, chipped tea cup of instant coffee as memories glide to the surface.

'We lived in lots of different places there but are now settled in Southhall. Near Heathrow.' Nostalgia swamping him as he spills milk onto the silvered tin serving tray.

'We have a nice house with a garden and Laila, my Mum, spends at least three or four hours working in the back garden everyday.'

I try to picture her pottering amongst English flowers in an English climate but fail.

I cannot conjure the Laila I know into such an alien setting.

I wish she was here to tell me what has happened since we last met in the Peshawar house.

We were expected.

My husband's cousin, Najaf and I.

Armed guards let us into the compound and pointed the way to a building separate from the main one.

The high, nail studded, wooden door swung open into a large, airy space with Laila sitting regally on cushions on a raised dais at the far end.

An unexpected sight.

Unveiled and smiling.

Dressed in embroidered *shalwar kameez*, brown hair in a neat plait over one shoulder.

She rose to welcome me and Najaf, a plump Punjabi, backed away in shock.

Afterwards he told me how amazed he had been.

'*Bhabi*, I have only met Afghans in Quetta. Men not women and I didn't expect a welcome like that. Not by a woman on her own. I didn't like it that you were coming to an Afghan place at all *Bhabi* but I had promised *Bhaijan* that I would look after you in Peshawar and that is why I went with you. The Afghans in Quetta would cut your throat if given the slightest chance but these ones are different!'

He was honestly amazed.

Now Laila, in a terraced Southhall home with little Gulshan, grown now, living a life I have left far behind.

She used to write to me, first from Peshawar, then Haripur when she was transferred to a refugee camp there, then again from Peshawar. Lamenting life as a refugee, hating Haripur and its heat, not really liking Pakistan and yearning for Kabul.

I wrote back, wanting to leave Scotland for Afghanistan, then working in the Sultanate of Oman before finally settling in Pakistan.

Thinking about it now, we have, in many respects, changed places, swapped lives although I have never lived in London.

'I went to school there as soon as we arrived. I'd been to school in Peshawar and Haripur before that and we used to have trips to Murree and Nathia Gali,' Farhad reminisced.

'I went to college, to do computers, in London too but got into a bad fight with a gang of Indians and had to leave while I was in my final year so didn't qualify.'

The scenario is not a new one.

Too many races, too many languages, cultures, customs and religions in small places.

Too much competition.

Inter-national.

Inter-racial.

Inter-tribal.

Inter-acting.

Inter-spersed.

Inter-rupted.

Interned in narrow stratas of society where they, mostly young men but sometimes girls too, eventually implode or explode as the case may be.

I have the distinct impression that Farhad is suffering an identity crisis.

Struggling to be a 'proper' Afghan while his 'being' wanders the streets of far away London.

He is the walking wounded.

A war child struggling to find his peace and his place in the scheme of things.

'After leaving college,' he continued, tracing designs in his tangled hair with outspread fingers, nails bitten to the quick, 'I worked in bars, even as a bar manager. It was a bit rough at times but,' after a meaningful pause and a wry, rather nervous grin, 'It was okay'.

He sounds like a naughty boy, caught in the act, trying to justify his actions, and I think, my impression is correct.

Poor Laila must have hung her head in shame.

'As you know, my Dad was killed in the war in Afghanistan and since then I really look up to my uncle, Anwar. He's a wonderful person. The kindest person I've ever met.'

I am not so certain of this but, then again, I hardly know the man.

'I came to Kabul six months ago. During the winter and Anwar lets me live in this house and look after it.'

I surmise that Farhad has probably been 'sent' to Kabul.

Banished from London in the hope of him finding salvation, or salvation finding him, in this, his homeland.

A case of Anwar to the rescue?

'Just after I arrived in Kabul I met a girl. The sister of a friend and I felt that this was it. You know what I mean Banafsha? Straight away I just knew that here was the girl I want to spend the rest of my life with. I told Anwar about her and he insisted that everything be done properly. Afghan style. So he sent someone to the girl's house to speak to her father. All above board and correct. After negotiations we got engaged two months ago and intend getting married in another couple of months or so.

She is a wonderful girl. I hope you can meet her while you are here.'

I hope so too and wish them well.

Perhaps she will turn out to be Farhad's saviour in disguise.

'I really miss London you know,' he continues, helping himself to more coffee at a rate which promises to empty the jar before the day is done.

'I miss the pubs and clubs. My girl would enjoy them too. I can't take her out and about in Kabul yet which I feel sad about. There are a few proper bars, serving alcohol, here, one of them run by two Americans, but only to foreigners or Afghans with British, German etc. passports. Not locals. I miss my Mum too but we talk on the phone most days.'

Like so many 'returned' young men Farhad needs to find work and asks for help which I cannot give as I don't know anyone here myself.

He, like many others, only wants to work with foreigners, not Afghans, as they pay more and the 'benefits' are lucrative too.

'Even though I didn't finish my education,' he stresses in a naive manner, 'I could work as a translator or in some administrative position. I would work real hard Banafsha. Make something of myself. Not be dependent on my uncle.

Make my mum proud of me but it has to be with foreigners. Working for Afghans is a waste of time and energy. Mostly they are just shit and will shit on you if you let them.'

Strong words from a mixed up guy who reminds me more and more of my old friend Lawrence, minus Buddhism, who, brilliant as he was, still ended up in a Glasgow gutter.

I don't know if he has managed to climb out.

Farhad is an echo.

More western than Afghan although he claims to have refused British nationality as he doesn't want to surrender his Afghan one. Instead, he has a permanent British visa stamped into his Afghan passport.

'Lots of other Afghans have taken British nationality,' he says. 'They have forgotten Afghanistan but I won't do that.'

Is he trying to convince me, or convince himself?

– II –

The jangling tune of his mobile phone sends Farhad scurrying outside into the neglected garden where the reception is clearer.

I sip my coffee and wait.

9.30 a.m. Still wondering if each and every passing car I hear is going to be Anwar, come at last to greet his guest.

'When are you coming to Kabul Banafsha?' he had asked on the phone when I finally tracked him down. 'Come straight to the Stadium.'

That place of *Taliban* atrocities and nightmares.

'My home is your home. Let me know exactly when you will arrive.'

I am here but...where is he?

A visit to my parents. October 1994 if I recall correctly.

Out for dinner with two of my three sisters at a countryside hotel in Lancashire when my father, men had been omitted from the event, came rushing in to tell me that someone from the Afghan Embassy had phoned and would call back at 10 p.m.

A quick drive back to be there in time.

Wondering where on earth the 'someone' had got my parents' phone number from, and more to the point, how did that 'someone' even know that I was in UK?

The phone rang right on schedule and a voice from the past asked, 'Banafsha. Is that you?'

Dust Motes – 7

'That funny little man in pajamas,' as another old friend, Maisie, in the Highlands of Scotland, called him in amusement as she ripped the ring-pull off yet another can of lager, her young son, Douglas, watching in resignation and knowing, that unless I made something for him before I left, it would be baked beans, spooned straight from the tin, for supper…again!

Hashim Sharife, short and square, working at the Afghan Information Centre in Peshawar back in 1983 when I dropped by to interview Professor Syed Majrooh, the renowned Afghan intellectual and poet who was assassinated a few years later when such political murders became a common event in that city, rival *Mujahideen* factions routinely attacking members of the 'opposition'.

Originally from the northern city of Mazar-i-Sharif, Hashim had been with the Afghan Agricultural Bank in Kabul prior to making his way to Pakistan as a refugee along with his wife.

He requested my home address and telephone number as I was leaving the office to head back to my miniscule room at Jan's Hotel, explaining that he hoped to be taking up residence in UK shortly, courtesy of a British Council programme and would then be in touch.

Surprised, and I admit, doubtful about his move, I gave them to him and was astonished when he contacted me, from Cambridge, early the following year.

A staunch nationalist, determined to return to Afghanistan once conditions improved, he intended to improve his education whilst he had the chance.

He visited Scotland over an Easter long weekend and completely failed to understand why I couldn't get time off from my newspaper position to show him around.

I did manage one day though and happily drove him from The Black Isle on the east coast, just north of Inverness, to Achiltibuie on the picturesque west. As we travelled along the side of Loch Broom towards Ullapool, he innocently asked about the numerous, huge ships anchored there and almost choked when I explained that they were all Russian vessels, 'Klondikers', in for the fishing and not very popular at all with indigenous fishermen following this trade.

'Why don't they do something about them?' he asked, cracking his knuckles, sounds like gunshots emitting from the warmth of the traditionally Afghan pattered, hand knit, woollen gloves he was wearing.

Expertly surveying the scene of tranquil Loch Broom, mountains on either side of the glittering finger of unruffled, sun-kissed sea, he quickly worked out just how many missiles were needed and the locations from which they should be launched in order to sink the entire fleet in seconds!!!

When we stopped for fish and chips in Ullapool I kept my fingers crossed that there wouldn't be a Russian sailor in sight.

There wasn't but, amazingly enough, Hashim managed to find a Shetland wool scarf which matched his Afghan gloves to perfection.

We then drove on to Achiltibuie and went for a walk on the beach where we discussed the situation in war-torn Afghanistan and what he would do when peace came.

It was the first time he had seen the ocean which he found menacing at first.

Running backwards and forwards in alarm as waves crashed onto the shore, he made a most unusual picture, dressed as he was in his traditional *shalwar kameez* and flat *pakol* hat.

We corresponded for about a year after that, right until I left to work in Muscat, the Sultanate of Oman, when we lost touch.

Now, almost eight years later, the phone call out of the blue.

'Banafsha. This is Hashim. How are you? I bet you are surprised to hear from me.'

Obviously I was.

'There are some visitors to the Embassy from Afghanistan,' he explained. 'After work was completed we all went to Wali Khan's home for dinner. He is the ambassador you know. Well, after we had finished eating we sat around talking and someone mentioned a journalist from Scotland who they knew. I told him that I also knew a Scottish journalist and had even visited her there and that her home was full of pictures and maps of Afghanistan. I also told him that I had been present at one of the fund-raising lectures she gave. Imagine…we were both talking about you!!! Here. He wants to speak to you.'

Hashim handed the phone over to the mystery man before I had time to ask where they had got this number from and how they knew that I was visiting UK.

'Banafsha,' said the voice, driving coherent thought completely out of my already confused head.

On official business in London.

He would visit me in Scotland the following week.

The date to be confirmed.

It was Anwar!!!

– III –

Farhad rushed back in, in 'whirlwind' mode, phone still clutched in his hand.

He has to go out, do a 'couple of things'.

Will be back for lunch and then, if Anwar hasn't arrived, will phone him and 'check'.

If Anwar isn't able to come, then Farhad will take me for a drive in the old city, 'lots of photo opportunities', maybe at 2 or 3 o'clock.

I make myself yet another cup of coffee in resignation.

This is ridiculous!

Half an hour later it's all change…or charge…typical Afghan style.

I remember it well.

Sitting around waiting, for hours, even days on end and then suddenly everything happens at once.

Farhad rushes back in, announcing, 'Okay Banafsha. Let's go to the Stadium and try to see Anwar.'

The car, Telabaz's Toyota Corolla, is covered in dust, as is everything else in Kabul including my sinus.

No wonder women wear *chadars*, *burkhas* and what look like dust coats.

I don't blame them one bit.

My *chadar*, tightly wrapped around my upper body and head, protects the lower part of my face from the sandpaper wind.

It will have to suffice.

As we leave the driveway, I finally pluck up the courage to ask the question which I came to Kabul to ask.

So afraid of the answer that I had bitten my tongue until now.

I felt that I would get a more definite answer from Farhad than from Anwar.

Taking a deep, steadying breath, I prepared myself for the worst.

'Where is Gul Ruz?'

I didn't know if he was dead or alive.

'Oh! Banafsha. Why didn't I think of it. I'll phone him right now,' Farhad answered, simultaneously starting to press the numbers on his tiny mobile, easing out into the traffic and changing gear.

'Is he in Jegdalek?' I managed to ask, relief flooding through me in a tidal wave.

'Where is he?'

Farhad nods his head as his call is answered.

Chats away in an unintelligible flow of Dari.

Tells me.

'Gul Ruz was in Jegdalek for a funeral. He just heard, early this morning, that you are here. He is on his way right now and should reach Kabul in about half an hour. He is coming straight to you and is inviting you to his home for dinner.'

Farhad appears rather taken aback at whatever it is Gul Ruz has told him.

I am not.

A full twenty-one years since we last saw each other face to face.

Nineteen years since I got married and the letters stopped.

I smile to myself knowingly.

My hero would never let me down.

– IV –

The traffic comes from everywhere at once.

It is supposed to drive on the right.

It just drives.

Huge trucks stick in the centre.

The yellow and white taxis actually seem better behaved than their Pakistani counterparts although Kabul boasts of one of the highest traffic accident rates in the world.

Kabul is smaller than I anticipated, or so it appears at the moment as I haven't seen much of it.

Other than Russian built apartment blocks buildings are one, maximum two storey, the city is prone to earthquakes.

Lying in a dust bowl encircled by mountains, distant peaks still snow covered in May, this is a city of illusions.

Peace, tension, silences, noise, alternate with each other in kaleidoscopic fashion.

Kochi nomads play flutes as they graze fat-tailed sheep on grassy road verges.

A group of giggling children, boys and girls in neat uniforms, play outside a school.

Bullet holes, sprayed over an entire apartment block announced 'Microrayon'.

Other bombed out buildings that Farhad, as a relative newcomer, doesn't know the name of and I doubt if he is even interested in such mundane matters.

He just knows that most of the damage was done during the fight for Kabul when different factions of *Mujahideen* tore each others' throats out in a frantic struggle for power, this, followed by even more fighting between the *Mujahideen* and the *Taliban* when the latter came to town.

I am studiously trying to make sense of what I see.

My mind is elsewhere.

'Dear Miss Pam Morris,' Gul Ruz wrote to me in Scotland, December 1983.

> We passed a very tough time in November, because a big Russian force consisting of hundreds of tanks, dozens of helicopters and fighter planes attacked our front. We resisted for a few days and finally we were unable to resist. This force remained ten days in Jegdalek, burnt our centres, food, medicine and everything. Killed our horses and cattle. Then after about ten days they left our fronts. In this battle 20 tanks were destroyed, 700 Russians were killed and one helicopter gunship carrying Russian advisors was shot down.
>
> By the grace of God only two *Mujahids* were martyred we are from God and to God we shall return.
>
> As ever,
> Gul Ruz

The figures quoted are not accurate.

A big number is more important than a small one.

It serves to illustrate what it felt like, what it looked like.

Not what it actually was.

It is not a lie.

Not a mistake.

It is a soldier's impression.

A *Mujahid*'s truth.

A few months later it was:

> Dear Banafsha Khomar!
> *Asalam-Alaikom*. I wish you good life and health. When I pray, I ask Allah for your health.
> Thank you very much for your letter, I received that. You have written that you don't have news about me. You are right, because I am usually in the front in Jegdalek.
> This year we had again some problems in the front, because Russians again came to Jegdalek. But this year we were in better condition than last year. We had more problems with food. Two days we ate plants. But in the fight we are better than Russians.
> I hope to see you again sometime in Peshawar or in Jegdalek. *Inshallah*. I remember, when we return from Tora Ara and we had lunch with Qazi—yoghurt.
>
> Please write me.
Your Gul Ruz.

By 12 June 1985:

> My Banafsha Khomar *Asalam Alaikom*!
> Thank you very much for your lovely letter, I received it. You are always in my heart. I am sorry, that I am writing you late. Just yesterday I arrived in Peshawar from front—Jegdalek. I am very happy to write, because my letter can see you soon than me.
> I am very happy for your new job in Oman. I hope to be near and see you soon.
> Please be careful, because Russian are working and they are not sleeping. KGB is very active and strong but Allah will watch over you.
> I remember the day we went to Tora Ara, it was special day. I remember all the time you spent in Jegdalek. When I go to Tora-Ara, always I remember you, but you aren't in Tora Ara.
> I am waiting to see you soon and go to Tora Ara again.
>
> All my love
Your faithful freedom fighter
Gul Ruz.

Letters from Anwar were completely different in nature:

My dear Miss Pam Morris
Here, everything is going well. If you have heard anything about the Russian's success, it is a sheer lie.

Sincerely yours,
M. Anwar.

12 May 1984:

Dear Pamorice

First of all I would like to wish you the best in life. Secondly, here is some recent news about the *Mujahideen* in Afghanistan and especially in Panjshir Valley.

As you know the Russians started their offensive in Panjshir in late April. For quite sometime we didn't have any news from there, but about four days ago we received the following report: In Feraj, Panjshir—the *Mujahideen* have killed and wounded many of the enemies' soldiers and have captured many different types of weapons.

Also, in Abdara and Burjaman Panjshir, the *Mujahideen* have captured about 900 armed men and killed 200 Russians and Parchamies. Of this 200 people who were killed about 90% were Russians. According to the reports the commander Ahmed Shah Massoud is fine and he is doing his works according to plan.

In Anamak-Salang, the *Mujahideen* have killed a lot of the enemy's people and captured many different types of weapons. Also, the report says that the *Mujahideen* burnt about 60 oil tankers of the enemy.

In Herat, the *Mujahideen* have also caused many casualties of the enemy and the enemy has lost many men in the process.

These were some of the highlights that we have gotten from inside Afghanistan. At the end I wish you a good time.

Please keep up your correspondence.

Very truly yours,
Anwar.

5 August 1984

Dear Pam Moris

The situation in the battlefield at Jegdalek front is under our control and we are thankful to God.

The Russians are on the defensive sides with not much of moral. I will return to Jegdalek in the very near future.

I hope to see you some day.

Sincerely
M. Anwar

Farhad screeches to a halt at the notorious Stadium, better known as a public execution ground in the days of the *Taliban* than as home to the Afghan Olympic Committee which it now is.

The façade is squat, brown, ugly.

A few tattered trees hang on to life at the roadside.

Brown with ingrained dust.

Not green and healthy.

I can sympathize with them.

I feel the same way.

– V –

Inside, the corridors go on for ever.

The entire building hums with activity.

The ghosts of the murdered and their murderers linger on in cracks in the cement walls.

Brown paint not dried blood.

Male and female voices float around.

People rush past us, arms full of top heavy paperwork.

Telephones ring in shrill demand to be answered.

The office of 'President of the Olympic Committee for Afghanistan and Director of Physical Education' is protected by an ante-room bursting at the seams with people, computers and a Kalashnikov-totting guard in camouflage gear guarding the heavy wooden door which leads to the inner sanctum.

Recognizing Farhad, the guard waved him through.

'Back in a minute Banafsha,' he said over his shoulder. 'I'll just see if Anwar is free.'

The guard did a double take.

Eyebrows meeting his hairline, black beard wagging furiously as he jumped startlingly to attention.

It was embarrassing.

'Please,' he instructed me, 'take my chair.'

Gesturing towards it with the barrel of his gun.

I didn't feel I had any option so sat in green plush splendour whilst the other occupants of the room unleashed a barrage of questions.

Far too young to have been in Jegdalek when I was there, he still knew an awful lot about me and happily filled everyone in.

'Banafsha was on *Jihad* with Mr Jekdalek,' he explained in fast flowing Dari.

'She wrote that book, *The Gun Tree* about *Jihad*. This is the first time she is coming to Kabul. She is married to a Pakistani and lives in the mountains somewhere near Murree.'

Heads nodded, men of all ages, some in *shalwar kameez* but mostly in shabby suits, tried not to stare.

Others greeted me politely.

Everywhere I looked, people tried to pretend that they hadn't been examining me in minute detail.

It was most disconcerting.

A group of five Turkish architects, arriving for an appointment, were swallowed by the inner door.

Three people were disgorged.

Nervous tension made the blood drum in my ears.

The waiting felt endless but it was only a mere five minutes or so until Farhad head-nodded me inside.

– Anwar –

An intricately carved, folding, wooden screen, placed directly inside the door, stopped me in my tracks.

Momentarily disorientating me, as it would anyone else who didn't expect it to be there.

It was a major step inside from the ante-room.

A small space where the next in line could wait until Anwar had finished dealing with whoever was in front.

'Come Banafsha,' Farhad ordered, as if he was presenting me to royalty.

'Anwar will see you now.'

Stepping around the screen, pausing at the sight of Anwar ensconced behind acres of polished wooden desk, deep in conversation with three men perched on the edge of their chairs before him.

Face to face with Anwar after ten years.

It was a shock.

A rather urbane, middle aged 'gentleman', smartly dressed in European style, greying hair, bald spot, reading glasses balanced on the end of his nose, fatter, smilier, but definitely Anwar.

Dismissing the men he rose to greet me.

Crossing the plush carpet with neat, quick steps.

Almost like a ballet dancer.

Professional wrestling training coming to the fore.

Hand extended in friendship.

'You know him?' transferring his grin from me to Farhad, sensing an 'Afghan' joke which promptly backfired.

'Banafsha remembers me being stung by a scorpion in the camp in Peshawar,' Farhad told him, still amazed at this fact himself.

Anwar was delighted but...before we got any further, a radio team arrived for a lengthy interview so he sent me to have tea at the conference table with the Turks.

Nice table.

A huge polished wooden oval with a matching oval hole in the centre.

I've never heard Anwar talk so long before, not in any language at all.

The interview, in Dari, concerned, amongst some other generalities, Afghanistan's hopes in the upcoming Athens Olympics plus the construction of a new gymnasium which accounts for the plans spread out on the table by the Turks.

Apparently one of them also designed this comfortable, if ostentatious, huge office, big enough to hold a major banquet in.

Araucaria trees in fancy pots adding a touch of nature to the otherwise overly ornate surroundings.

The fancy plaster mouldings on the ceiling could have come straight from Versailles!

Black tea in fancy glass cups embellished with bunches of grape vines and flowers.

Plates to match.

A serving platter, divided into four segments, foil wrapped sweets, *kish-mish*, walnuts and pistachios, none of which I dare touch as my throat is so irritated by the wind-blown dust outside.

The interview goes on and on.

Questions being fired by a young man and a young woman in rapid succession.

Farhad wanders back outside.

I sip my scalding hot tea.

Decide to photograph Anwar and unpack my cameras.

I select the Nikon FM2 with its speed light.

The speed light falls in bits as I try to attach it to the camera.

Batteries clatter onto the table.

Everyone looks.

I blush furiously and pack it away, taking out a standby Pentax, with a telephoto lens instead.

I feel Anwar's eyes watching me as I circle the room, searching for an angle.

I find one and watch in amazement as Anwar's face turns a sickly kind of green.

Trying to concentrate on the interview he is inexplicably nervous.

I adjust the telephoto distance, trying to catch his expression and then realize.

He thinks I'm going to assassinate him!

He is remembering what happened to Ahmed Shah Massoud.

Guns and bombs hidden inside journalists' cameras.

He is uncertain of me.

Uncertain of my intentions.

I'm shocked.

I take some photographs anyway.

Return to my tea.

He visibly relaxes.

Who is afraid of whom?

Scotland in 1994.

Full of apprehension, I met him at Inverness airport.

He entered the small building filling it with menace.

A medium-sized man with over-large shoulders, warning eyes and heavy black beard.

Green combat jacket bulging with muscles.

Dark trousers.

Dark sweater.

A walk that warned 'Don't tangle with me!'

Nobody did.

The way miraculously cleared before him.

Even I felt like running away.

Out into a borrowed Volvo car.

The drive past Inverness, over the Kessock Bridge and onto the Black Isle where I was staying with a friend.

Anwar, occasionally grunting in reply to a pleasantry.

To a question.

Being his normal, uncommunicative self.

Silently taking in the scenery.

The Highlands in autumnal dress.

Scotland at its best.

Suddenly demanding, 'Where is a hotel?'

'I have prepared a room for you in the house where I'm staying,' I told him. 'There is no need for a hotel.'

'Who is in this house?'

'An old friend called Henry.'

'Is he your relative?'

'No.'

'Then you cannot stay there either.'

'My husband gave his permission for me to stay there. He knows where I am and can phone.'

'You should stay in a hotel also.'

'No. You should stay in the house.'

We argued, or rather I argued while Anwar sat as immovable as one of the distant mountains.

He refused to change his mind.

I took him to a hotel in Fortrose.

Organised his room and then took him for a refreshing walk along the beach.

'It's too cold,' he complained.

'It's too rough for walking.'

He scowled at the panoramic view, seascape, landscape, fleecy clouds scudding, windborne across the late afternoon sky.

Turned his back on everything.

Shut out his surroundings.

Turned, hands stuck deep into jacket pockets.

Launched an inquisition.

'Why were you in Peshawar at that time?'

It took me a minute to realize what he was referring to.

'I was there for a family *shadi*. You know that. You attended.'

He nodded…reluctantly, so it seemed.

I was puzzled by his manner, his tone of voice.

'What do you know about Arif? His murder?'

Stunned.

Looking at him in disbelief.

What was he accusing me of?

'I didn't know anything at all until I came to your house in Peshawar,' I told him, horrified at what he appeared to be inferring.

'Laila told me about it.'

He grunted.

Flinched as a seagull screamed raucously overhead.

'How many times have you been to Afghanistan?'

'Only once, with you, you know that.'

'Only once? He queried.

'Yes. Only once.'

He searched my face.

My eyes.

Concentrating hard.

I was a hare frozen by the glance of an eagle.

A chicken facing a snake.

Petrified of the solemn stranger challenging me on a Scottish beach.

Seconds ticked into minutes.

Minutes into hours.

Time was suspended.

The cold, salt-laden wind brought tears to my eyes.

Or...was the wind responsible?

It could have been fear.

He seemed to be struggling with something inside his head.

Searching through memory banks, stored information.

Whatever he found there, whatever confusion he waded through, he didn't say but finally grunted, half smiled, walked away.

We got back into the car and drove, conversationless, to Henry's house where I was cooking dinner.

I, full of apprehension.

Wondering why he had asked such questions.

Wondering what he was doing here at all.

We had certainly not got off to a good start.

This was Friday, he was staying until Monday.

What on earth was I going to do with him and...why had he come if he was going to be like this?

Had he come to accuse me of murder?

Dinner, a celebratory salmon stuffed with pomegranate seeds, almonds and herbs was not the happy reunion envisaged.

Henry did his best.

Telling humorous stories in a broad Stirling dialect which Anwar had trouble in comprehending.

Henry was in the middle of decorating his cottage living room.

Anwar was fascinated by the process of hanging wallpaper.

His eyes followed Henry's every movement.

The stories passing him by.

He pulled up close to the fire, stirring coals with a heavy iron poker.

I washed the dishes in a vain attempt at relieving pressure.

'I will go to the hotel now,' announced Anwar in a voice which dismissed alternative persuasion.

It wasn't even 8 p.m.

I dropped him there.

Spent a sleepless night.

Returning for him at 9 a.m. the next morning.

He was out.

Walking on the beach when I found him.

I was wary.

Hurt.

'Would you like to visit the West Coast?' I asked. 'It's very beautiful.'

'I need to return to London,' he said.

'Today if possible.'

Surprised, relieved, I drove into Inverness to get his ticket changed.

No seat available until Sunday afternoon.

We were both disappointed.

A drunken woman beggar accosted him in the street.

He winced.

I drove him to the West Coast after all.

A tape of my favourite music, instrumental, Alasdair Fraser, 'Sky Dance', fiddle, piano but always the dancing, soaring fiddle.

My 'West Coast' music.

A personal tradition to listen to on the long mountain road from Dingwall to Ullapool, Achiltibuie or Gruinard Bay which is where I was heading now.

We talked, briefly.

'How is Gul Ruz?' I picked up the courage to ask.

'Okay,' spoken with abrupt finality.

Mountain peaks and moorlands flashing by in a haze of greens and browns.

A desolate landscape.

A desolate feeling.

'Where are all the people, the houses?' he asked. 'The land is empty.'

'The English drove them out over 100 years ago so that they could fill the land with sheep. More profitable,' I told him.

Painting word pictures of the infamous Highland Clearances.

Pictures he could understand.

'Why didn't the people fight?' he asked with raised eyebrows. 'Like we fought the Russians.'

'They were poor people. Some did fight for their land, their homes and those that weren't killed were forced, at gunpoint, onto ships bound for America, Canada. They had no option.'

'They could fight the English now. We could help them,' he observed with a wry grin.

It began to rain.

A persistent Highland drizzle.

Despite a pearl grey mist rolling in from the ocean, I managed to point across Little Loch Broom to Scoraig, a roadless peninsular, a handful of houses, painted windmills for power, where I once lived.

'You lived there!' battling a gale to keep on his feet, seeing an impossibility.

A hardship which he couldn't comprehend.

'Yes. After I came back from Afghanistan,' I explained.

'I needed to hide myself away.'

That...he understood.

Yet another silent drive to the airport on Sunday.

Both of us still on the defensive.

Arriving early.

'Let's have coffee while we wait,' I suggested.

'No Banafsha. You must go now.'

'I'll wait until your flight is called Anwar,' the hospitable thing to do.

'No. You go now. No waiting. Time does not come twice. Go. We will meet again...if it is written. Go.'

I went.

This is a very different Anwar in front of me now.

The interview finally drew to a close.

I waited...as normal.

Four men marched into the room.

Three of them quite young, the other one older.

Three of them in smart business suits, the other in a crumpled *shalwar kameez* and waistcoat.

The group of three presented themselves at Anwar's desk, he rose to greet them.

The other man just stood.

He searched the room with nervous eyes.

Searched the faces of everyone present.

His piercing gaze rested, momentarily on me then moved on.

Checked out the Turks from head to toe.

Came back to me.

Eyes colliding with eyes.

It was Gul Ruz.

END OF PART TWO

PART THREE

Time swings on a pendulum.

Tick-tock.

Tick-tock.

Jegdalek–Kabul.

Jegdalek–Now.

1983–2004.

Gul Ruz–Anwar.

Anwar–Gul Ruz.

Swimming through quicksand.

Somehow I cross the floor.

'Hello. How are you?' says the well-remembered voice.

'Fine,' he answers himself before I have time to speak.

A strong, firm grip takes me by the hand while eyes still rake the room, relentlessly searching.

Eyes the colour and bubbling consistency of my Aunty Ada's butter toffee as it simmers on the stove.

Soft brown with pinprick explosions of golden light.

He speaks English!!!

No. He doesn't.

Just a phrase he has picked up.

His eyes bounce on and off Anwar then back around the room.

Totally out of place, out of time in these plush surroundings.

A mountain man come to the city.

For some inexplicable reason he conjures up an image of Giovanni Drogo, the central character in *The Tartar Steppe* by Dino Buzzati.

Farhad reappears like a genie from a tarnished lamp.

'Banafsha,' he says. 'Gul Ruz wants to take you to his home. He says to tell you that you are quite safe with him. He has taken a Japanese journalist to his home before. He says to tell you that you have nothing to be afraid of.'

Afraid!

Afraid of Gul Ruz!

Afraid of my hero!

Never!

Anwar is watching the meeting, the exchange, with hooded, predatory eyes.

His dealings with the three men in front of him put on temporary hold.

I can't tell what he is thinking.

Farhad, not knowing better, jumps the gun.

'Banafsha is going with Gul Ruz,' he innocently informs Anwar who is not looking at all amused.

'He will drop her back later.'

The three men start talking, negotiating again.

I nod in Anwar's direction seeking permission to leave.

He nods an abrupt dismissal.

I have been hijacked.

I have no say in the matter.

– II –

Following Farhad and Gul Ruz back along the endless corridors and down echoing stairwells, I pause to take a quick photograph of the grassy arena which the stadium holds in its encompassing grasp.

A huge portrait of Ahmed Shah Massoud holds dominance over a sward of under-repair grass and running tracks.

I try not to imagine the numberless amputations, the executions which took place here.

Try not to picture the blood.

The ghosts of *Taliban* victims scream at me in anguish.

They don't want to be forgotten.

I calm them with a quick prayer then rush to catch up with the two men, in deep conversation, gesticulating wildly in every direction except mine.

We pass the curious eyes of receptionists, of heavily armed, patrolling guards, emerge into the dusty wind and sunshine, walk towards a row of parked cars.

After returning to Scotland from Afghanistan, to peace from a war, I often daydreamed, when things were not going well, that Gul Ruz would ride out of a brilliantly painted West Coast sunset, throw me across his horse and spirit me away.

Gallop me back to Jegdalek.

Gallop me back to a different time, a different life.

Now here he was.

Much older.

Much wearier.

The longish thick black hair streaked with premature white completely replaced by a short, hennaed, crop.

He had obviously had a 'bad war'.

There was no horse.

Instead of four legged transport there was a travel stained Toyota Corolla, the ubiquitous car of Kabul, to which he gallantly opened a rear door.

A sweaty *shalwar kameez* lying on the seat was hastily brushed aside revealing a highly polished, well maintained Kalashnikov.

No horse…but still Gul Ruz.

Taller than I recalled, he folded himself carefully into the driving seat, still engaged in rapid, serious conversation with Farhad.

I didn't have a clue what it was all about.

The pulsating Dari far too fast for me to pick out individual words.

Everything flowed together, melded into a rhythm of sounds, carried me back to Jegdalek again.

To sitting beneath '*The Gun Tree*' listening to the voices of *Mujahideen* flowing around the courtyard after a supper of hot *nan* with sugar sprinkled on top.

Sipping green tea whilst trying to understand what was being planned, who was going out to ambush a convoy, which men were being sent onwards to Panjshir and when.

To not understanding what Anwar said in reference to me.

Knowing it was I they were talking about as he kept looking in my direction, amusement in his voice, something totally different in his eyes.

Feeling the beginning of fear.

The only woman in a valley of 1,500 men.

To Gul Ruz reprimanding him.

To Anwar laughing and commenting again, throwing a 'hot' look in my direction.

To Gul Ruz reaching behind himself.

The glimmer of cold steel in the lamplight.

Sharp metal flashing in his hand as he half crouched to rise.

The others reacting in individual ways.

Two trying to take the knife away.

Others eagerly leaning forwards towards a fight.

Anwar saying something else unintelligible to me.

Gul Ruz hissing from between clenched teeth.

Legs bent in a half crouch.

A panther ready to spring.

I paralyzed, trying to make myself invisible against the rough bark of the suddenly dangerous tree.

Anwar realizing that Gul Ruz was serious.

His face changing as he tasted the explosive tension in the camp.

Laughingly saying something else that I didn't comprehend.

Diffusing the tension.

Gul Ruz sitting back down.

The knife disappearing.

Tea being poured.

Back to 'normal'.

– III –

Edging the car carefully out into the traffic he spoke softly in Dari.

I still didn't understand.

I asked if he spoke Urdu now but he didn't and I still don't speak Pashto.

It was just as it had always been except for the letters, written for him, mine translated for him by others, the only time we had communicated 'directly'.

'Banafsha-Khomar' he slowly said, shaking his head from side-to-side as if to clear his vision.

'Banafsha-Khomar.'

It was then that I noticed his hands.

Fingers melted together.

The car had manual gear shift.

A right-hand drive in a left-hand drive country.

To change gear he needed to use his right hand, not as badly damaged as the left, which meant taking his right one off the steering wheel, crossing it over his left which rested on the wheel, to complete each difficult manoeuvre.

I tried to ask what had happened but he couldn't explain.

Just repeated 'Banafsha-Khomar', and shook his head.

– IV –

I am astonished to find that 'home' is a top floor apartment in Microrayon.

I don't know what I had envisioned but it certainly wasn't this.

Unlike in the majority of Pakistani apartment blocks, the stairwells were quite clean.

No *paan* stains for one thing.

Most of the windows on the stairs were without glass, those on the first two floors with chain-link mesh nailed or wired into place.

Our footsteps echoed hollowly as we climbed.

His front door, a heavy metal sheet with a tiny eyehole for those inside to inspect new arrivals.

Such security is necessary.

Inside, the apartment is quite spacious, resembling, in many ways, the Karachi, Seaview apartment my husband and I lived in when we returned to Pakistan.

The walls are all a chalky turquoise blue with scratches and scrawls in the paint—Russian noughts and crosses, the aftermath of *Taliban* torture or just children's mischief?

I can't decide.

The floors and *takhts* are carpeted, mostly machine made in Iran and one handloom from Herat.

A dark blue and brown '*Zanjeer*' affair.

As in Farhad's home, elephant's foot predominates.

Two television sets, one tuned to an Indian movie, one in the living room, the other in a guest room.

A highly gold braided Afghan Army Commander's cap, incongruous on top of a glass fronted cabinet.

People and children everywhere.

Comfortable and noisy chaos.

Gul Ruz has two wives.

One here, Marina, and the other, his first wife, in the village of Bagrami not too far away.

Marina, plump, laughing, in a long skirt and blouse of stretchy, black synthetic material spangled with gold lurex thread.

Worn over a modest black *shalwar*.

She welcomes me with a hug.

He also has twelve children, six boys, six girls equally divided between the two women.

A tiny baby is being swung in a white painted wrought iron cradle by a little girl in plum coloured bellbottoms and long matching shirt.

The little girl is one of his, the baby, his eldest son's who has a giggly, fair-skinned wife.

The eldest son, Khair Muhammad, was 13 when I was in Jegdalek all those years ago.

'When I am martyred then he will take my place,' Gul Ruz said then.

Khair Muhammad is on his way here.

He speaks English and Urdu as well as Dari and Pashto.

He will be our translator.

Another lady, Lailoo, in a full skirted green *kameez* and matching *shalwar*, heavy black *burkha* thrown back over her head, sits crying.

Her eyes red and swollen.

She is the wife of Gul Ruz's elder brother who is seriously ill.

A stroke combined with asthma?

He can't speak or hear but wants to participate in everything that he can see.

He is ushered away into another room.

Gul Ruz and his brother are in *shalwar kameez*.

A boy of twelve, Darwish, Marina's eldest child, lounges in front of the television in jeans and T-shirt.

The past and present at a glance.

Darwish is learning English at school and also speaks some Urdu.

'Banafsha,' he yells in excitement. 'Do you know Kiko? She is a Japani. She gave me this watch.'

He holds his wrist out for inspection.

'She had *shadi* here.'

Darwish just can't keep still.

He is bursting at the seams with life.

Khair Muhammad arrives.

Sombrely clad in dark coloured *shalwar kameez* and jacket...I am certain that I have seen him before...but where?

I soon learn.

Two or three years ago, after lunch in Nathia Gali, watching television with friends.

A BBC Channel 4 documentary, John Simpson bravely tracking down remnants of *Taliban* in Northern Afghanistan.

Jabal Sarooj if I recall correctly.

Surrounded by translators and bodyguards.

One of the translators reminded me of Gul Ruz.

He was not quite as tall, skin tone a little darker.

The hair was Gul Ruz's Jegdalek hair although it obviously wasn't Gul Ruz but...there was something about the eyes.

It had been Khair Muhammad who is now in his father's regiment of the Afghan Army.

Commander Gul Ruz, Jamiat-i-Islami de Afghanistan is now a Commander again.

I learn later that both the apartment and the army positions were made possible by Anwar.

Accommodation and work are at a premium in Kabul.

They are almost impossible to obtain.

His regiment patrols the road from Kabul to Jegdalek, over the historical Lataband Pass where thousands of British and Indian troops, along with their camp followers, were brutally massacred during the 'Retreat from Kabul' which marked the end of the First Anglo-Afghan War in 1842. Only a doctor, Dr Brydon is recorded to have survived, arriving wounded and starving in Jalalabad, though there were others.

It seems ironic to me, Gul Ruz's regiment guards the very same power line, from Sarobi to Kabul, which the *Mujahideen* targeted in the war against the Soviet Invaders.

'The more things change, the more they stay the same'.

Time is of the essence.

I take out my tape recorder and get down to work.

It is expected of me.

GUL RUZ

'I was born in the mountain village of Jegdalek approximately fifty-three years ago,' he begins, after fortifying himself with a cup of green tea poured from a very large, flower stenciled thermos which he keeps at his side.

'I grew up there like my father, his father, and his father before him. We were farmers. We were content. We had a good life before the Russians came in December 1979.

'We still have a house and lands in Jegdalek but the house was completely destroyed by bombardment of the Russians. So now we have our land but no house. All of the houses in Jegdalek are destroyed. The entire village is destroyed. You know that. You were there and you saw it.'

I nod in agreement and ask about landmines.

'The area is full of landmines', he says sadly. 'We can still go there because we have some ways. If we use these ways we can go. We can't work in the fields to plant crops. This is too dangerous. It is not possible to be a farmer there at this time. There are no NGOs working in that area and no assistance is there. At this time, maybe, I think that about 80 or 100 families have come back but it is not enough. Jegdalek is a very big area and had a very big population before the war but many of our people are still in Pakistan as refugees. They haven't come back because they know that there is no school, no roads, no power, it is very difficult. They don't have a hospital there, no doctor. Even if there were such facilities then the people still cannot grow their crops because of the mines. These are the basic difficulties for us. If there were more people in Jegdalek now then maybe some help would come but the people will not come until help is there. Until the mines are taken away. Until they can make a life again,' he shrugs his shoulders in resignation and lets his eyes see pictures of life 'before'.

I also recall Jegdalek, although I have never seen it as a thriving, bustling, farming community, only ruined and deserted.

Prayer flags fluttering over the graves of martyrs.

Blackberries and apricot trees flourishing along the dried up riverbed...geese flying in a 'V' overhead in clear blue, autumnal skies.

Cultivated fields overgrown and neglected.

A watermelon struggling to survive.

Shrapnel embedded in the trunks of ancient mulberry trees, the sap trickling down trunks, red and sticky...like blood.

Tatters of cloth, dented pans, broken stoves, broken homes.

The detritus of a people hurriedly fled.

Jagged mountains rising from the narrow valley floor.

Unexploded bombs in pomegranate orchards.

'After you left from Afghanistan, from Jegdalek, then I continued fighting there, against the Russians and then against Najibullah until we entered Kabul in victory in 1992. When we first came to Kabul we thought that fighting is finished but this was not the case.' He looks very forlorn and I hope that he is not feeling hurt by my questions.

Sometimes the past is better left buried.

'There was too much fighting with other groups of *Mujahideen*. This was a very tough time for us. At that time, in Kabul, I was always with Commander Anwar and I was in command of a regiment. I was also assistant to Commander Anwar like Jegdalek Front time. We stayed in Kabul for about four years until *Taliban* came and then we left. All the world knows about *Taliban*, and as you know, there is a small area called Panjshir and we go over there to strike against *Taliban* for about five more years. Now we are very thankful for forces of America and forces of ISAF (International Security Assistance Force). They have come here to help us against Al-Qaeda and *Taliban*. They want to kill Al-Qaeda and *Taliban* and also we do.'

'Why do you not like the *Taliban*?' I ask.

'First, there is a difference between *Talib* and *Taliban*. They are both Muslim. In Islam *Talib* means a good guy, a guy who learns the historical and religious and poetry and *Talib* is very good man in our villages. These people who were and still are fighting in Afghanistan under the name of *Taliban*…they get the name of *Taliban*, they get the advantage of the name of *Taliban* but these were and are not *Taliban*…they are traitorous groups. They think that if they get the name of *Taliban* then all Muslim people will depend on them but this is not the case. At the beginning we thought to welcome them as we didn't know that they are not the same as our *Talibs*. We didn't know they were bad people. At first we didn't realize this but then we came to realize that they are terrorists and must be destroyed.'

The family members who were in Kabul when the *Taliban* took the city, first fled to a once lush agricultural and grape-growing area north of the city known as Shomali Plains.

'As you know, when we went to Shomali as refugees it was very difficult for us': A fact which Marina later expands on.

'But the situation was like that. Food was very hard to find.' He obviously doesn't like to hark back to this period of time and I don't press him.

His face is drawn and haunted.

'In Panjshir, Ahmed Shah Massoud who first was leading the fighting against the Russians, was now collecting more people to fight against *Taliban* so we went there to join him. This was the Northern Alliance. It was a very difficult five years, but thanks to Allah, we survived and we succeeded against *Taliban*.'

I wonder, was he happier to be a farmer than to live in the city?

'Your question has two ways,' translates Khair Muhammad sitting cross-legged at his father's feet concentrating intently. 'The first, I like the previous period but I like now also because…you know about the "Front" time and since that time I am working for Afghanistan, for the people of Afghanistan. Even now I am working on safety of power supply and Lataband road. At this time we are also very tired of fighting.'

The exhaustion and disillusionment of twenty-three long years of war, the first ten years against the Russians who retreated in 1989 leaving Najibullah to run the country for them and still the fighting continued; then the *Mujahideen* infighting after they triumphantly took Kabul in April 1992 only to be ousted by the *Taliban* in 1996 with remnants of *Mujahideen*, mostly of Tajik, Uzbek and Hazara decent and a smaller number of 'Pathan' elements, then re-grouping to form the 'Northern Alliance' under the leadership of Ahmed Shah Massoud until he was assassinated, when victory was clearly in sight, on 9 September 2001 just two days prior to the horrendous attacks on the World Trade Centre in New York and the Pentagon in Washington.

This was followed, on 7 October 2001 by the beginning of Anglo-American intervention and a month long American campaign of bombing, the likes of which the country had never experienced before.

The *Taliban* hung on in Kabul until 13 November 2001 when they abandoned the city overnight and the Northern Alliance took over until 22 December 2001 when Hamid Karzai was sworn in as the leader of an interim government, his nomination agreed during complicated international negotiations held in Bonn, Germany, a couple of weeks before.

But...still the fighting continues, remnants of the *Taliban* and other malcontents carrying out more and more attacks on both foreign occupation forces and the newly re-formed Afghan Army and police forces.

No matter how long and hard one looks into the tangled web of Afghan and foreign intrigue there is still no actual peace in sight.

The proverbial light at the end of the tunnel is currently not visible.

I do not think that this was what Gul Ruz was, and is, fighting for.

'Is your father happy that American troops and the International Security Assistance Force have come?' I asked Khair Muhammad. 'You see, when I went to Jegdalek my impression of Afghanistan and of your father's life was very different than now. What I can see, after so many years of fighting, is that he has a home in Microrayon but cannot go home to Jegdalek. He cannot go home to his land. The land he fought so hard to keep.' I gesture, probably angrily, certainly in confusion, around the room. 'Is this what he was fighting for?' Realize that I may very well be misunderstood so attempt to continue in a softer voice although my emotions are running high, 'From the beginning he wanted a free Afghanistan but Afghanistan is not free. You have American control.'

'You are right Banafsha,' Gul Ruz concedes via his son. 'But the first thing is that when we were fighting against Russia we thought that we would get a free Afghanistan and then we get Afghanistan.' He scratches his short hair in disgust, eyes narrowing as he forms the words to explain. 'For four years we are in Kabul, but as you know, some countries like Pakistan and Iran, they don't want a free and strong Afghanistan. So there were some errors. Then came *Taliban* and you know the story that we go to Panjshir for five years. Now we come back here. I don't think America will get Afghanistan. America and ISAF say that they have come here to bring peace and after peace they will give the kingdom back to *Mujahideen*. Just like that. They only come here to bring peace not to get Afghanistan.'

He heaves a deep sigh, expelling his breath out from between tightened lips as he pours more tea for the three of us.

'Why should America come here to make peace?' I ask. 'It has no reason to do that. America has come here because they want to establish bases here. They want control of oil, gas, minerals. They want to use Afghanistan as a base into Central Asia. They want to control Afghanistan, Uzbekistan, Tajikistan. They want to control Afghanistan, Pakistan, Iran. They want to control the whole world.' I am getting carried away on the strength of my convictions but can't stop the flow. 'Before they came to Afghanistan they had no bases here. They are using Afghanistan and when they are finished they will leave. Then what will happen?'

I feel like shaking my hero to wake him up.

He doesn't like what he is hearing and replies, getting more belligerent by the second at the prospect of what I have said being true, 'If you study the history, first time English came, they wanted oil, gas, minerals, ruby mines. This was not good for us so we gave them a fight and they go away. Similarly with Russians, and now America has come here. If America do something like this...then we do something else.'

The fire is back in voice, the spark in his eye.

I caution, 'America, with their sophisticated weapons will be very difficult to get rid of!'

'What you say is maybe two things and the answer is one,' he continues now lounging back against his cushions and narrowing his eyes. 'The British Empire came here and started fighting and Afghanistan was very weak. During Russian time Afghanistan was also very weak but now that the Americans came here to support us with our freedom, to help us win our freedom but...if America it wants to keep Afghanistan then we CAN do something.'

On a calmer note I ask, 'How do you feel when you see the foreign soldiers here now? When I got off the plane and saw them in the airport I didn't like it. They were controlling, it didn't feel as if they were there for the people's safety. They were very threatening.'

'You are right Banafsha but the Americans and ISAF are here to ensure that there is peace in Kabul. They also discuss with us, how is peace in Kabul, is it 100 per cent, is it 70 per cent. But...maybe they are not completely good people.'

'But Kabul is only one place Gul Ruz. There is all of Afghanistan to consider. How do you see the future? For you, for the children? What do you think the future holds?'

'At this time Banafsha it is very difficult to tell you 100 per cent about our future,' he concedes, whilst folding and unfolding his ruined hands.

'Now is the beginning. We have to see the programme of government, of ISAF. They make roads, they make schools or not. They make progress in agriculture, in import and export, in power stations or not. This is the beginning now. We can see the situation. I cannot say 100 per cent what is the future.'

'Many people who left and went overseas as refugees are now coming, or thinking of coming back to Afghanistan,' I query. 'Do you feel that they are changing the culture? Take television for instance. It shows different ways of dressing, different ways of many things. Even right now, on the streets and inside homes everything is changing. Becoming more western. Do you approve of this or did you prefer Afghanistan before the Russians came?'

'As you know, Islam is not a prison,' he straightens up, scrutinizes my face. 'If you are a girl or you are a wife then you can work. She can go to the bazaar to buy things. She can go to school. She can go to the mosque to learn Islamic studies. In a home a television is no problem. It is a thing of information not a problem. In the circle of Islam we can observe freedom better but people who have come from western countries, if they want to get the beer and other things, then we do not like that.'

On this note he points to my tape recorder, indicating that I switch it off.

I do.

He is impatient to ask questions of his own.

Twenty-one years is a long time after all.

He asks about my life after I left Afghanistan, after he ordered three of his cousins to escort me back to the relative safety of Pakistan when the Russians were advancing on Jegdalek.

After he stood and watched me leave…both of us silent then.

The questions of that time left unspoken, unanswered…even now.

It is difficult with Khair Muhammad as translator.

We both know this.

I tell him about Scotland, the Sultanate of Oman, Scotland again and now mountain life in Pakistan.

The type of life I envisaged him leading in Jegdalek.

We chat this way for half an hour or so and then he suddenly asks, 'Where is your husband?'

I realize that this was who he was searching, scanning the room for, back in Anwar's office.

'Did some agency send you to Afghanistan,' he continues, groaning aloud when I tell him 'No,' and realize that, if that had been the case, he may well have requested a fee...times are hard.

Darwish and a mass of other children rush in eating hot *nan* stuffed with green onions.

The aroma is delicious!

They have come to tell us that lunch is being served in another room.

Gul Ruz rises to his feet as more 'guests' have arrived and he must greet them.

I take the opportunity to ask Khair Muhammad about his father's melted hands.

'My father is a Commander in the Afghan Army as you know,' he explained. 'About fourteen months ago he was in Sarobi on duty. He finished his duty late in the night. He had wanted to come to Kabul earlier to reach the airport for some government occasion and he is late. On the way there is a car accident and the car burst into fire. That is how he suffered these injuries and many more.'

DUST MOTES – 8

I sense that, despite his co-operation, Khair Muhammad does not like me.

Resents my intrusion.

Trying to ease the palpable tension I tell him of the time his father spoke about him when we were in Tora Ara.

'He told me that you were 13 years old and at school in Pakistan. He was very proud of you.'

'Yes,' he reluctantly answers, his eyes almond shaped and luminous. 'I went to school in Peshawar and also in Haripur district. Now I am with my father in the military. The National Force of Afghanistan. Also, when I can, I work as a translator.'

I enquire more about his military work.

'Jegdalek belongs to Kabul province and you know that Sarobi has three power stations and Sarobi has two ways to Kabul.

'The Lataband way is the responsibility of my father's regiment which is named 904. We keep guard of the power lines from Sarobi to Kabul.'

He is obviously very proud of this, proud of his father too. I ask about the time spent in Panjshir.

'As you know, we have two homes. My father has two wives. At that time I was in Pakistan with my mother, my father's first wife. When we had no news of him for more than one year then I travelled to Panjshir to try and get information on how it is there and where is my father. This took me about three months and then I returned to Pakistan.'

'How did this feel for you? It must have been very hard not knowing about your father?'

'When I go to Panjshir at this time it is the first border between *Taliban* and *Mujahideen* and on this borderland I think this is the "murder-land". When I crossed this land I was very happy to see my father. I went to my father's home and was very happy to see my father alive. After this, I go to Mazar-i-Sharif and I look at all the people and I was very worried because all the people they think they are surrounded and it is not a good situation.'

'Weren't you afraid that the *Taliban* might catch you?'

'Yes,' he replied honestly. 'I was very afraid that they would conscript me and try to force me to fight my father. So, after sometime, I went back to Pakistan.'

'I sense that you are not happy with the current situation here Khair Muhammad. With the American and ISAF troops.'

'This is correct,' he admits. 'I try to tell my father but he will not listen to me. I am very concerned about our situation, about the conditions in the whole of Afghanistan. I do not approve of the Americans and ISAF. I do not trust them in the long term. My father gets angry with me if I say this. He refuses to listen. Perhaps he will listen to you.'

Marina comes to hurry us up before food goes cold.

'This is my new mother,' Khair Muhammad says. 'This is her home. I, my wife and children live with my mother in a place called Bagrami on the outskirts of Kabul but we come here very often.'

I wonder how he feels about the situation, the family circumstances and why he is so obviously wary of my presence here.

I do not ask.

– V –

The small front room, just to the right of the main door, contains Gul Ruz, Khair Muhammad and a man I do not know but who greets me with respect.

Lunch is laid out on a pretty cloth on the floor.

Traditional Afghan style.

We sit around the cloth on cushions of brightly patterned material.

The women and children will eat what we leave.

Another tradition.

Pilau rice, green bean and tomato *salan*, red bean *salan*, yards of *nan*, watermelon and gallons of green tea.

The men eat hungrily.

Gul Ruz silently adds pieces of meat to my plate.

An honour.

In Tora Ara it was lumps of potato which he transferred from his plate to mine.

'Why?' I asked then.

'Where you come from people like potatoes I am told.'

I didn't ask now.

I now know the customs.

This is how a guest is treated in Afghan and other similar cultures.

Over tea the men chat for a while.

Gul Ruz asks more questions about my life, my husband, my work.

Suddenly announces, 'Banafsha! I am now your *Bhaijan* and this is your home.'

He waves a hand around the room, sketching emotions in the atmosphere.

Khair Muhammad, sullen again at the translation, eyes brimming with something uncomfortable.

His father looks at me directly for a long moment...continues, 'Your *Bhaijan*. You can live here for as long as you like. You can work in Kabul. There is no charge for staying here as you are now family. You can have this room to live in. If you need anything, anything at all, then tell me and I will do whatever I can to obtain it for you. I am your *Bhaijan*.'

His eyes glitter as he lays his world at my feet.

Magnanimously offering all that he has.

'*Tashakkor*' I thank him in Dari.

Meaning it.

Recalling that magical day in Tora Ara yet again when we sat in the shade of a walnut tree festooned with guns.

When he scrutinized a handful of uncut rubies proffered to him by a roguish looking character who had appeared from the direction of the famous Jegdalek mines.

The *Mujahideen* still mined the rubies, stored ammunition in the hidden tunnels and caves.

Not looking at me directly, Gul Ruz handed me his choice of stones.

To examine I thought.

I did so then handed them back.

'No,' he told me, still looking away.

'The rubies are for you.'

Only then did he turn and face me.

Tiger's eyes boring into mine.

'The rubies are for you.'

'*Tashakkor*' I had told him then...as now.

'My father must leave for a short while,' says Khair Muhammad. 'He must attend a meeting of area commanders at the American Embassy. They have some projects to discuss. He will not be long. He will see you when he comes back.'

Gul Ruz and the other man leave...the women and children enter and eat the remains of the food.

Khair Muhammad has been left to translate if and when required.

He would much rather have gone with his father.

I sip my tea, trying to follow the chatter of the women.

Try to answer Rita...Khair Muhammad's wife as she lets loose a barrage of questions.

Admire Marina's new *shalwar kameez* which she has proudly rushed to don.

To staunch a fresh torrent of tears as Lailoo wails her husband's health.

I am utterly drained.

Emotionally exhausted.

I stand, for a minute or two on the miniscule balcony outside the kitchen, trying to revive myself.

Trying to put everything into perspective.

Kuchi nomad children herd their fat-tailed sheep between the war scarred apartment blocks.

A pile of stale *nan* in a box awaits re-use or re-sale.

I need space.

I need room to think.

I need to sleep.

'I will drop you back at Farhad's place now,' says Khair Muhammad, as if reading my mind.

Gul Ruz still isn't back but i know I will see him again so agree to leave.

Khair Muhammad has more important things to do than nursemaid me.

This is obvious.

As we exited the building Gul Ruz was on in his way in.

He looked disappointed.

A forlorn figure in a black cloth jacket with large, black cloth covered buttons.

Kalashnikov in one hand, a plastic bag containing two mangoes in the other.

I am ashamed by his pain.

In the car, Khair Muhammad tells me, 'The Americans have ulterior motives in coming to Afghanistan. Someone else said, "We thought they came to make us free but they occupied us instead," and I agree with this statement. It is true.'

Adding, with a challenge, 'This is also happening in Pakistan where both China and America are quietly doing the same thing that America has done to us.'

I didn't feel like debating the issue.

My mind overflowing with conflicting images, I didn't even notice where we drove, just realized, suddenly, that we were there and I could finally retreat into my den and collapse.

– VI –

Farhad emerges from his room as the *jali* front door blows to with a crash.

'Banafsha! I wasn't expecting you back yet. Is everything okay?'

'Everything is fine,' I tell him, although in my whirling mind it most certainly isn't. 'I just need to rest for a while.'

'I have arranged for my fiancé's brother to drive you around in the evening,' he tells me before I can enter my room. 'Naeem has gone off somewhere and I can't leave the house empty. He will come for you later.'

'Thanks,' I tell him, retreating into my room.

I lie comatose for an hour on the mattress I have chosen for my own.

Alternate between drifting and dozing.

Imagine that I can hear a woman's voice from somewhere close by.

Realize that it must be the television and drift again.

Get up to go and make tea and bump into another female in the passage outside.

Farhad can't go out.

Rubbish!

He has his fiancé stashed in his room!

He joins me for tea but doesn't mention her.

She is supposed to be invisible.

We chat for a while.

I am amazed that he has never heard of 'Dire Straits' despite a London upbringing.

'I have arranged a car and driver to take you around the city tomorrow,' he informs me. 'I would like to take you myself but I have some things to do for Anwar. Anwar is also very busy tomorrow but he will come when he can.'

He disappears and I see him escorting his fiancé to the car and driving away.

He is back in half an hour with Sabir, a friend of his and a battered black taxi.

'Sorry but I need the car,' Farhad says.

'Sabir is my fiancé's brother and he will accompany you. I have told him where to take you. He speaks Urdu so you won't have a problem.'

My Urdu is not all that good but I don't say so.

I will manage.

– VII –

As the sun goes down and even more dust comes up we drive into a nether world of distorted oncoming headlights, of bicycles wavering in a strangely fragmented dimension.

Ghostly figures emerge, re-emerge, completely disappear in the heaving gloom.

Men: Central Asian characters in 1950s suits, Pathans in *shalwar kameez*, old, young, healthy, crippled, smiling, leering, going silently about their business.

Women: Bundled up in dark coloured *chadars*, flowing headscarves, *shalwar kameez*, girls in tight jeans and figure hugging jackets all intermingled with gliding *burkhas* in pale blue shimmering through dust and light beams.

We are floating through a surreal movie.

An art form.

– VIII –

The taxi rattles and groans up a steep incline, bushes on either side, a manned police barrier solidifies in navy blue mist as we approach.

The driver switches on the interior light.

Harsh red illuminates us.

Armed police, three of them, stare and smirk.

They wave us through and I wonder what I have let myself in for now.

Alone with three strange men, in the dark, no one but the threatening police around.

The taxi climbs some more.

Wheezes to a halt on a windy plateau inhabited by the broken hulk of a building.

The city lights lay spread out at our feet.

Eddies of dust fill the air with sound.

The sighing of sand, the creak of something I can't identify.

'The tomb of Nadir Shah', says Sabir nodding towards the ruin. 'It was destroyed by *Mujahideen* when they took Kabul. There was much fighting then. Many people were killed. Many buildings destroyed.'

'I can't see it in the dark,' I tell him. 'I need to come back in daylight.'

'Yes,' he agrees. 'That would be better. There are millions of mines here.'

A police car materializes out of the deepening night.

I am extraordinarily nervous.

We climb back into the cab and head back into the city.

'There are some places you should see,' advises the bespectacled young man who is Sabir's friend.

What they show me is miles and miles of deadly razor wire, steel and concrete barricades, gun emplacements, armed watch towers with searchlights, menacing soldiers on the prowl, guarding their encampments, patrolling the perimeters of the world which they inhabit.

There are nightmare borders bearing signs such as 'No photographs. Anyone acting suspiciously will be shot'.

Apparently trying to take photographs of these camps which inhabit vast areas of the city itself as well as the surrounding countryside is considered a suspicious action.

I put my cameras away.

None of us want to be shot.

Convoys of armoured vehicles crash through traffic lights oblivious to anything except their own intentions.

They are terrifying.

The taxi inadvertently gets caught up, surrounded by Armoured Personnel Carriers.

I feel that the end has come.

These massive, featureless machines, threaten to pound us into the dust just by their presence.

Their engine fumes poison the dust laden air.

If anyone attacks them now we will be dead.

If someone has mined their progress we will be blown sky high.

'Pull over until they have gone,' I instruct the driver in a quavering voice. 'Please pull over. Now!'

Dust Motes – 9

The taxi driver comes from Baghlan Province in the north of Afghanistan and is more than eager to tell me his opinion of things.

'These Americans and ISAF soldiers are intimidating,' he earnestly informed me, spitting out of the open window as he did so. 'Why do they need to barricade themselves in from us? Karzai does the same. He hides behind American bodyguards. He hides from his own people. Though I really think, and so do many others, that he is really an American himself. He should go back to America and we should have a proper Afghan, a proper leader who is not afraid of us in his place. We need a strong man, a brave person, not this coward.' He spits again for emphasis.

He is a thin, hooked nose man with a half grown beard and slicked back dark hair.

Probably in his mid-thirties, his prominent cheekbones and slightly slanted eyes hint at Uzbek or Mongol ancestry although he is not Hazara.

'I fought the *Russ* with *Mujahideen* when I was young,' he proudly explained. 'We didn't have many weapons in our village but we did what we could. When the *Taliban* came though I finally left for Pakistan and spent five years working as a butcher in Peshawar. Better to be a butcher there than get butchered at home!'

'In Kabul I can only find work as a taxi driver, nothing else, and my village has no work either,' he says in disgust. 'Too many mines in the fields. No work anywhere. I don't like it in Kabul though. We all had enough of war and now we get this,' he indicates yet another convoy approaching from the opposite direction.

Maybe the same one returning.

I don't know.

I just want them to evaporate.

'The Americans are the worst,' he continues. 'Closely followed by the Germans. They beat people for no reason. They use their rifle butts whenever they feel like it. Just last week someone I know left his home to go and open his bakery, like he did everyday for year upon year. Even in the Russian time. Everyday he had to walk past one of these camps where the soldiers hide behind their razor wire and concrete. He wasn't doing anything, just walking past, not even looking at them as that can be dangerous, just looking at the floor and walking. They stopped him though. Beat his brains out with their fists, rifles and kicked him down with their big feet. They didn't stop until he was red meat in the dust. Then they just left him there by the roadside and no one dared go to pick him up until they had gone away. He was buried that day. Now his wife and eight children have no support. An honest man going to earn an honest living and that is what they do. Foreigners!' he managed to spit again before putting the car into gear and edging back onto the road.

'He is right you know,' agrees Sabir's friend. 'These things and much more happen all the time. No one is safe in Kabul. No one is safe in whole Afghanistan. We will not be safe until these intruders leave. They are not wanted here.'

We drive back into the city centre, the 'tourist area', Chicken Street where people are strolling, window shopping, admiring western style wedding dresses in white lace, pale green, pale pink and lavender concoctions flanked by ornately decorated wedding cakes, tier upon tier of icing sugared splendour.

They look obscene after what I have just seen and heard.

I have had enough.

We pick up a mountain of *mantu* and head back to the villa.

'No,' insists the taxi driver when I try to pay him.

'No money. You were with *Mujahideen*. I cannot take money from you.'

I insist but he still refuses.

'Tell the people that we are having problems still,' he instructs. 'Tell them that we want the Americans to go away and take Karzai with them. They are not wanted here.'

Ending, with a verbal flourish, 'Anytime you need a taxi I will be there. Take you anywhere. Show you everything. No pay' and he roars off in a blast of purple exhaust fumes mouthing purple prose in Dari as he goes, taking Sabir's friend with him.

– IX –

I shared the *mantu* with Sabir and Waliyat Khan, the guard, though they ate in the guardhouse and I in carpeted and cushioned splendour.

Farhad came back, bringing more food and his fiancé who, surprisingly enough, was obviously going to spend the night.

'You should get some rest Banafsha,' he suggested.

'You have a long day ahead tomorrow but you don't need to get up before 9 a.m. as the car will come at 10 a.m. when the morning traffic jams are over with.'

He disappears into his room where his mysterious fiancé is already ensconced.

Returns in five minutes to add, 'Banafsha. I forgot to tell you that Anwar is very busy but he will make sometime to see you soon.'

I have heard this before!

END OF PART THREE

PART FOUR

– I –

Dawn comes slowly after a restless night of low flying helicopters.

Of the crack of gunshots fragmenting star-shine.

The rumbling reverberation of APCs.

Of tanks outside the gate.

Echoes of Jegdalek raising the hair on the back of my neck.

Fear in the pit of my stomach.

Disjointed dreams.

Nightmares.

Tangled confusions surmounted by Gul Ruz on a rearing white stallion, a sprig of lavender in his hand as Anwar shoots him down and I obliterate Anwar with a fragmentation grenade, pulling the pin with my teeth as tears flow from panic-stricken eyes.

An unseen hand flinging rubies in my face.

Sharp edges cutting.

Blood flowing.

Gul Ruz reassembling himself from a billion tattered bits.

Gathering up the rubies and offering them to me.

The rubies turning into the pomegranates which I once picked from the orchard surrounding the bombed out shell of Anwar's Jegdalek house, carrying them back to the base camp in my travel stained black *chadar*; rolling them across the lamp-lit courtyard where they came to rest at their rightful owner's feet.

To Anwar grinning in triumph in Gul Ruz's direction.

To myself trying to dissolve into the rough bark of '*The Gun Tree*'.

Frightening myself awake.

Shivering and hating the endless moaning of the Parwan Wind which blows for months on end.

It roars out of the Paghman mountains north of Kabul.

Rampages across the province which bears its name to whistle through this tortured city.

It lowers the temperature and raises the dust.

I am sure that it can drive people insane.

The 'Mistral' does.

– II –

If the pulse of this phoenix city is anywhere, it is in the voices raised in song, in play, from a close by children's school which boys and girls attend at separate times.

The boys first, girls later.

Infact, schools all over the city and beyond are humming with activity, the eagerness to learn, to drink up information: new knowledge lighting up small faces with a beacon of radiance.

There is hope.

There is also hope in the beat of Indian film music from the footpath stall selling cassettes and cigarettes which leans against the street side of the guardhouse wall and which filters into where I dip stale *nan* into hot, black coffee, idly wondering what the same vendor would have stocked, if anything, during the *Taliban* time when these things were completely banned.

The intrusive, shrilling demanding ring of mobile phones, yet another sign of the times.

The ringing thud of hammer on nails; the slap, slip, slop of wet cement on bricks as yet another building rises from the ashes.

The myriad sounds of a city being reborn.

The dusty atmosphere is electric.

The wind whirls itself dizzy in lunatic delight.

It has seen this city devastated, wiped out, obliterated, rebuilt, more times than we humans care to recall.

It has shrieked its defiance down the centuries.

Whirled sand and grit into the eyes of Mongol horsemen, down the barrels of British rifles, into the rotor blades of Russian, now ISAF helicopters in triumphant glee.

It tosses the dust motes of centuries towards an increasingly turbulent future and waits; resting in autumn and winter mountain passes for spring and summer when it roars through the country once more.

It is roaring with uninterrupted savageness this morning.

– III –

10 a.m. on the dot.

A sturdy Russian jeep, large, white, very high up and punctured by rusting bullet holes ricochets into the driveway, tearing a hole in the flapping *purdah* curtain in the process.

The driver, in smartly pressed army greens leaps out of one side. Sabir, in jeans and T-shirt doing his best to imitate Tom Cruise, jumps from the other.

Jeep doors crash closed as Waliyat Khan, Kalashnikov over his shoulder struggles against the grit filled gale to close the entrance gate behind them.

Farhad emerges to greet them and I hear his girl rattling around in his den.

The jeep belongs to the 'Olympic' fleet of vehicles, and like Cinderella, comes with a time limit.

'It must be back by 4 p.m.,' stresses Farhad, turning to let the wind blow his hair out of his eyes and regretting the movement as particles of dust momentarily blind him.

'Also, I will need to go out then and Naeem will be leaving and I can't leave the house empty.'

I still don't understand the fear of an empty house.

'Waliyat Khan will be here,' I reassure him.

'No. He is going with you. It isn't really necessary so don't be alarmed. Just a precaution.'

My *chadar* flaps in the wind, *kameez* threatens to blow inside out, even my *shalwar* is ballooning as I struggle to get myself and my camera bags into the back of the jeep.

Sabir rushes to help, wordlessly making clear that this is one of his roles for the day.

Translator, guide and assistant all rolled into one.

A holiday atmosphere pervades the boxy vehicle as we roar off to explore.

First stop is the devastated tomb of Nadir Shah in daylight.

The police barricade is even more heavily manned than on the previous evening.

It appears ominous.

Threatening.

Until, that is, I spot a guard in combat fatigues watering a bed of blazing scarlet geraniums with a hosepipe, rifle slung over his shoulder as he concentrates on his task.

A small nursery, green-netted on an adjacent roundabout, offers more geraniums, colourful dahlias and pots of petunias along with an assortment of young trees and shrubs.

Another sign of hope.

Of growth and new life.

One side of the road leading up to the mausoleum is home to a demining organization, and so, I was assured, there are no mines left in this vicinity but...maybe they had missed one...maybe it had my name written on it.

The moving finger writes; and, having writ,
Moves on: nor all thy Piety nor Wit
Shall lure it back to cancel half a Line,
Nor all thy Tears wash out a Word of it.
                    (Rubaiyat of Omar Khayyam—Fitzgerald, First Edition)

What will be, will be.

Kabul is the heaviest mined city in the world after all.

Afghanistan the most heavily mined country on the planet.

It is estimated that over ten million landmines were buried here during
the Soviet occupation, a number that vastly increased when American
planes plastered the country with cluster bombs, many still unexploded,
when they moved in to force the *Taliban* out.

People step on them everyday.

Are blown sky high.

Maimed.

Killed.

It could, quite conceivably, happen to me.

The jeep growled to a stop at the edge of a rough area which serves
as a car park and from which one gets, under calm conditions, a
panoramic view of the city below and its surrounding mountains.

Today however, the dust haze blots most things out.

A crowd of clamouring children selling sweets surround us as we
climb out.

Surprisingly…they don't beg.

This is not Pakistan.

'Only take photographs of the tomb and areas of Kabul which do not
contain any army or ISAF camps,' Sabir advises. 'I will show you
where to look. Looking anywhere else can be dangerous. There could
be trouble.'

Obediently, I turn to concentrate on the shattered buildings, and just as I clicked the shutter for the first time, two intimidatingly large four wheel drive extravaganzas screeched to a halt, ISAF troops pouring out in an instant.

What was happening?

What had we done?

I hastily hid my two cameras under my flapping *chadar* and looked away.

I hadn't done anything!

Waliyat Khan moved in on my right hand side, Sabir on my left.

Hamid had elected to stay with the jeep.

On guard.

The atmosphere was full of tension.

There was no need...the soldiers had come sightseeing too!

The mausoleum of King Nadir Shah, who ruled Afghanistan from 1929 to 1933 when he was assassinated by a protesting student, must have been incredibly majestic before the *Mujahideen* finally captured Kabul and the infighting between the various factions erupted to destroy vast areas of the city.

Abdul Rashid Dostum, who changed sides, from Soviet to *Mujahideen* and back again with regular frequency, was holed up in the once magnificently blue domed building during this vicious civil war, his motley band of troops, derogatorily nicknamed '*Gilam Jam*' or 'carpet thieves' keeping him company. They faced Gulbuddin Hekmatyar, dug in, in the mountains across the way, Professor Rabbani's Jamiat-i-Islami, which then included both Anwar and Gul Ruz, in the Wazir Akbar Khan residential district and others all around. Dostum, from this strategically important vantage point rained armaments down on his enemies, obviously being targeted in return.

During this unforgettable period, the warring factions of *Mujahideen* literally shot hell out of each other and everything and everyone else in-between.

The shell-shocked remnants of King Nadir Shah's mausoleum will never recover from this catastrophe though a lone, struggling, pale pink hollyhock, valiantly sprouting from a crack in the paved flooring suggests otherwise.

However, the King's actual tomb, although scarred by bullets and shrapnel, is intact, and even had fresh flowers on it when I was there.

In an underground crypt, directly below, lie the remains of the recent monarchs of Afghanistan and their families including Queen Homaira, wife of former King, now 'Father of the Nation', Zahir Shah, who died in Italy at the ripe old age of 86 whilst waiting to rejoin her husband in Kabul after an exile of thirty years.

As I entered the crypt, stopping to pray as is my custom on entering any burial ground, the caretaker was first shocked, then delighted, as were both Sabir and Waliyat Khan who had completely forgotten that I am a Muslim!

I declined a proffered trip through the encircling catacombs, which when walking around the ruins above them, one must be extremely wary of falling into as they are in a badly dilapidated condition, full of rats which I saw running around along with scorpions and snakes which I thankfully didn't.

Walking, half bent against the wind, back to the waiting jeep, I caught glimpses of the legendary Bala Hissar Fort in the dust laden distance, 'Out of bounds,' I was informed by a sombre Sabir, 'Mined and dangerous.' I certainly saw the notorious Stadium where Anwar would be hard at work in his plush office and a huge hospital complex which, according to Waliyat Khan, was almost without doctors.

'A nice visit now,' announced Sabir, as he helped me to change a roll of film in my camera. 'A surprise!'

The three musketeers grinned conspiratorially at each other.

In true Afghan style...no one was going to give the game away.

– IV –

Whizzing in and out of heavy traffic, bracing myself for the collision which didn't come, trying to take in the sights.

Shells of war ravaged buildings gapping dangerously in-between their miraculously undamaged neighbours. A totally different picture than the ones given by the media who would have the world believe that there is absolutely nothing left standing.

The incorrect impression that Temur and his hordes had been to town.

True, accommodation is in extremely short supply.

Sheets of plastic, squares of tin and cardboard filling holes in shattered buildings, creating places in which people, long term city residents rendered homeless through no fault of their own, internal migrants from the still un-safe countryside, refugees returned from countries such as Iran and Pakistan, struggle to make themselves comfortable, fight to survive in anyway they can.

Without running water.

Without bathrooms.

Without electricity connections.

Totally without privacy they live as best they can, face each new day, each trial and weary tribulation with a proud mixture of patriotism and hatred.

Pathan, Tajik, Turki, Uzbek, Kochi, Hazara; from Kabul, Mazar-i-Sharif, Kandahar, Herat, Jalalabad, Zabul, Zazi and all the places in-between; from cities, towns, villages, mountains; forest dwellers, desert people, nomads; Afghan despite their ethnic differences, languages, dialects, cultures, customs, mode of dress, right down to the taste and ingredients of the food they eat.

Afghan but angry at how they are forced to survive now that the war has been won.

Now that the 'good fight' is over.

Now that peace is supposedly with them again.

Bitterly disappointed with a government which offers them little, if anything at all.

Disillusioned with a President who does not dare to walk the streets in which they live.

Living in dread of yet another freezing winter without adequate shelter, without enough food to feed their starving children, without money to put warm clothes on their backs.

The war widows, the war wounded, the orphans.

They inhabit a totally different Kabul than the Anwars, the Farhads, even the Waliyat Khans of this multi-level city.

Live in a separate universe from Laila in her London garden, Gulshan with her studies, Hashim in the bank.

These people are the real dispossessed.

Echoing ancestors down through the ages, the flotsam and jetsam, the dust motes on which countries eventually depend.

Are they the reason why Farhad will not leave the house empty?

Would they, or others like them, simply move in, take over, fight to death to have a reasonable roof over their heads?

Could one blame them if they did?

I think of the thousands who have not yet returned and maybe never will.

Happy in their American, European or Asian homes.

Satisfied to have decent jobs, full stomachs, access to education, to good doctors and hospitals, the comforts they would find it difficult to do without now that they have become accustomed to them.

To cars, washing machines, fridges, televisions, fashionable clothes and pastimes, prosperous futures, security if they work for it and if, and to this there is no guarantee, war doesn't follow in their migratory footsteps.

War erupts where it will.

Where the wind carries it.

Dust Motes – 10

'Actually I was born in Pakistan,' admits a baker from behind the busy counter of his Pakistani store. 'My family is from Kandahar but left there when the war against the Soviet Union got too much. Our home was destroyed, our lands not safe and as so many relatives and friends had already come here that my parents decided to come too.'

Extremely plump, spotless white shirt bulging over the belt of his smart black trousers, he continues in a distinct American accent, breaking off now and then to shout orders in Dari to unseen staff in the back, 'My parents settled in Quetta. They still had money so rented a nice house and both I and my brother were born there. Then they got refugee status in California so we went there for a few years. We even got American nationality but please don't tell anyone that as it could affect my business and my property interests here. My mother and brother are still there. They like it. But…my father, he was not happy there, he only wanted to return to Kandahar. As soon as the *Taliban* were ousted he got on the very next plane to Pakistan and brought me with him. I didn't want to come. I wanted to stay where I was.'

Waiting while he served yet another Saturday morning customer, I wondered why he had elected to set up business in Pakistan, and once the lady had left with her bags of aromatic garlic bread, fresh French sticks, apple pie and pizza, I asked him.

'Well,' he almost whispered, conspiracy in the air, 'I also have Pakistani nationality and I can actually earn more here than in America. Here there are not so many good bakeries but in California there are many. I even earn enough to send money there for my mother.'

I ask about his father.

'He is in Kandahar now. When he brought me back we went by road to Kandahar, passing through Kabul on the way. I hated every minute of it. It was dangerous, the journey was difficult, the food bad and the heat awful. Here I have air conditioning. Anyway, when we reached Kandahar we found that we have no home there any more. Everything was lost so we came back to Pakistan and I set up this business but my father was still unhappy. He couldn't settle here so he went to Kandahar again and is still there trying to sort things out but, in his heart, he knows that the family will never return. Only him. He is an old man now. His heart is broken but he needs to be in Afghanistan so that is where he is.'

Another customer comes in followed by four more.

I pick up my cardboard carton of cheese and spinach patties, a bottle of cold mineral water and emerge into stultifying heat of a Pakistani high summer wondering at the multifariousness of it all.

– V –

Sabir insists that we stop across the road from bullet scarred 'Shah-do-Shamshira' mosque, the mosque of 'Two Swords,' still beautiful if covered in pigeons.

The pigeons, like those at 'Rauza Shahe Welayatmaab', the 'Shrine of Hazarat Ali' in Mazar-i-Sharif and other holy places in Afghanistan, are claimed to carry the souls of martyrs so are fed and pampered.

This interesting, two storey mosque on the Kabul river, in what can now be considered the city centre proper, was constructed in the 1920s and stands on the original site of what was one of Kabul's first mosques. Legend relates that, on this spot, an early Islamic hero was killed in a battle against Hindus who were protecting their temple which then stood close by. The unnamed hero, as far as I can ascertain, rode into battle wielding a sword in each hand, this despite already having lost his head earlier that day. He was reputedly one of the first Islamic warriors to arrive on the Kabul scene and this battle, fought in the early seventh century, represented the arrival of Islam in the country.

Trying to get a clear photograph of this commanding structure proved a little difficult as intruding convoys of ISAF vehicles kept getting in the way and I knew better than to get them in the picture, inadvertently or otherwise.

Sabir, meanwhile had not called a halt for me to see the mosque but to disappear in search of waterproof markers with which to catalogue my used rolls of film.

This was not the 'nice surprise' that he had in mind.

As we edged back out into the fast moving traffic I spotted something which I can best describe as a prime example of 'America takes over Kabul',...four labourers pushing and pulling a huge wooden cart bearing an absolute mountain of Pepsi bottles incongruously topped with a watermelon!

My three companions were really getting into the swing of things now, even gruff Hamid managed a comment or two and suggested possible photo opportunities.

A huge single deck bus with three cars on its roof, 'Saves petrol,' said Waliyat Khan with a grin.

'*Gilam Jam,*' Hamid shyly throws in, nodding towards a once extensive row of stone built buildings of which, spaghetti western style, only the façades remain.

'There. There. We go in there,' instructed Sabir bouncing up and down on his seat like an eager child.

'Good fun,' he told me. 'Enjoyment place.'

The zoo.

They had decided to take me to the zoo!

Hard hit after twenty-three years of war it is somewhat smelly, particularly near the pig enclosure, but throngs of people, including Waliyat Khan with his Kalashnikov and Hamid who had abandoned his precious jeep for the duration, obviously relish the pleasure of walking around and taking in whatever sights there are left.

The pigs, donated by China in 2002 along with two lions, two bears and a wolf, were being vastly enjoyed by a group of young boys who were racing around grunting and oinking at each other whilst these naked looking, pink beasts rolled malevolent red rimmed eyes in their general direction.

It was clearly evident that the staff is trying desperately to maintain the zoo properly, see that the animals and birds are fed, the gardens re-planted and the place kept clean but it is also obvious that they face an uphill task.

The monkey enclosure, an island surrounded by water, surrounded by a low concrete wall was of interest to me personally as I have never seen monkeys swimming before. They could escape if they wanted to but are on to a good thing so why bother?

I have never come across a monkey climbing a frame constructed out of combat gear webbing before either.

The wolves and foxes appeared rather mangy, the famous bear, 'Donatella', couldn't seem to make up her mind whether or not to go into her den but kept on heavily swaying up to the perimeter of her cage, snarling at the delighted observers then swaying away again. She was highly agitated by something, perhaps the wind and dust storm that was definitely brewing, but, if it was the same bear who recently hit the headlines then her nose infection is now clear.

The other eight bears were far more co-operative and happy to perform tricks for pieces of watermelon thrown by the fascinated crowd.

The long-eared owls, with glowing amber eyes, were really something to see but a large chameleon in a too small cage was quite unable to defend itself from the long, sharp, prodding sticks of mischievous boys.

The elephant house and its sad inhabitants were destroyed by rockets during the civil war and the tomb of 'Marjan', the *Talib* eating lion tells tales all of its own.

Hundreds of people throng the zoo each day, thousands on holidays.

It serves its purpose.

More interesting than the zoo, to me that is, but not to my enthusiastic escort, was an area of land across the river which backs the zoo premises and where industrious men and women were hard at work growing fields of green onions, tomatoes, cabbages, aubergines and melons.

I hoped that the area had been thoroughly demined but no one seemed to know.

Empty plots throughout the city, even the gardens of doomed houses tottering in the breeze, are planted with all sorts of vegetables creating vivid splashes of greenery, fresh food, in the most unexpected of places and serving to emphasize the utter wastage of productive land in cities across the globe which concentrate on developing 'green belts' and amenity areas instead of essential, inner-city food supplies with which to counter inflation. Counter poverty and hunger.

Across the road from the zoo entrance, and acting as a road divider, is a beautiful strip of fruiting trees, shrubs, flowers, grass and running water which, according to Waliyat Khan, was funded by Anwar, a 'Pickernicker place' for the people to enjoy.

Anwar, it seems, has far more hidden faces than I ever would have guessed at.

Escaping from the zoo, much to the disappointment of my 'guards', was not exactly an easy task as they would happily have remained there all day but I had other, more serious, destinations in mind.

– VI –

An emerald green blotch on a sand grey hillside.

First, stacked houses, an endless deck of cards, then simply exposed rocks above and behind the reconstructed walls and archaeological remains of 'Bagh-e-Babur'—the 'Light Garden of the Angel King' (Peter Levi).

Gardens and the designing of them, was one of the numerous peaceable pursuits of the first Mughal Emperor Babur, great-grandson of Temur, perhaps better known as 'Tamerlane', the great Mongol who himself laid waste to Kabul, along with much of Central and Western Asia in his time.

Laid out in the middle of the sixteenth century, the six hectares of this once spectacular garden on the western slopes of 'Sher-i-Darwaza' mountain, are currently being restored to their former splendour by the Aga Khan Trust for Culture who are spending approximately three million dollars on the project.

Hamid, elected to guard his jeep this time, archaeological remains holding no attraction for him but both Sabir and Waliyat Khan were enthusiastic, happily shelling out the 2 Afghanis each entrance fee.

Scrambling over a dry ditch and up the rough, dusty incline from the roadside, I stubbed my open sandal-clad big toe on a piece of extremely sharp metal which imbedded itself instantly much to Waliyat Khan's horror.

'A butterfly bomb,' I had time to think in shock as he hastily and rather expertly, jerked it out, flinging it as far away as possible with eyes and mouth wide open.

Ignoring the dribble of warm blood I tensed for the inevitable explosion.

Nothing happened.

'Shrapnel,' announced Waliyat Khan in relief and we walked on.

The garden is on a series of terraces leading up to an under-construction restaurant which, when completed, will provide diners with a panoramic view of the city on a clear day.

Each terrace is being remade in its original Mughal style of flower beds, fruit trees and fountains, and when eventually finished, particularly when the people in charge can lay their hands on more than Calendula, Antirrhinum, Sweet William, Tagete, Zinnia and Canna plants, should be spectacular. The Privet hedges were in need of a trim and the grass beneath predominantly Apricot trees needed cutting but one cannot complain at the marvel which is being achieved.

Added to this is the most incongruously spectacular swimming pool, complete with diving boards and teeming with male swimmers, that I've ever seen. It is literally a shimmering sapphire of a pool suspended between earth, mountain and sky but I was unable to find out anything about it except 'Enjoyment'.

And, as if this wasn't enough, even further up the steep slope and a little to the right of this sapphire attraction is a cliff-backed, emerald green one, cool, inviting and fed by a gush of spring water emanating from the depths of the mountain itself. This is the ancient reservoir for irrigating the gardens and the spring, from which the mountain gets its name, one of the main reasons that Babur selected this site for what eventually became both his favourite garden and his personally selected burial site.

The sapphire pool has to be paid for, the emerald one, free for those brave enough to take the chill temperature along with the wrath of the gardeners if they are caught, was full of children in rubber tyre inner tubes having a whale of a time. I wished I could join them.

The tomb of Babur is a modest affair which oozes dignity and commands attention. He actually died in Agra, India in 1530 but had left instructions that his body be brought back here and that nothing should cover his grave so that the elements could beat down on it and wildflowers, another of his passions, perhaps take root.

Due to internal family strife, the usual of who would succeed whom, his request was delayed but his Afghan wife, Bibi Mubarika, eventually ensured that his dying wish was granted. His tomb was exactly how he wanted it to be until first, during the seventeenth century, Emperor Jahangir had a marble headstone erected and then, during the short reign of King Nadir Shah a marble slab was lain on the grave itself and this, in turn, was covered by a small pavilion.

Infighting between the *Mujahideen* was responsible for much of the garden's destruction, as were later predations by the *Taliban* who 'massacred' the ancient *chinar* trees standing between Babur's tomb and the delicate marble mosque, built by Emperor Shah Jahan in 1646, close by. The civil war destroyed the pavilion, exposing the tomb to the elements again, as Babur had wished but it also destroyed the beautiful mosque which is now being painstakingly recreated.

Babur's wife, Bibi Mubarika is buried close by him as are other members of his family including a son, a daughter, a grandson and a granddaughter.

I had a personal reason for paying my respects here.

According to my husband's family history, the family trace themselves back, first to the Kashgar Princess who was their grandmother, and through her, directly to Temur from whom Babur was directly descended.

Many years ago, in Muscat, the Sultanate of Oman, I had promised my husband's wonderful mother, Miriam Zamani, that, if I ever returned to Afghanistan, I would pray at this tomb. I was lucky enough to be able to honour my promise.

Palace ruins, off to one side of the garden, were in a deplorable and highly dangerous state though Waliyat Khan and Sabir both told me that even twelve years ago they were in good condition.

The civil war again.

As we searched, in vain as it was lunch time, for someone to further enlighten me about the ruins and the gardens, the Parwan Wind, which had been hovering around us all morning, kicked into action, telling us that it was time to go.

Racing back down to the jeep through stinging sand and grit-filled miniature whirlwinds we encountered a crocodile of teenagers, boys and girls, jeans, T-shirts, denim jackets, headscarves and back to front baseball caps, making their way upwards.

'How are you Aunty? Welcome to Afghanistan.'

Unknowingly jolting my memory back to 1983 when it was:

'Welcome to Afghanistan.'

'Are you a doctor?'

'Do you have any medicine?'

'You will tell the west what is happening here?'

'You will tell them the truth?'

'Tell them we need help.'

I did as they asked.

I was only a journalist.

No one listened.

– VII –

Darulaman Palace, standing on a small 'hill' at the end of the impressively long, straight and wide avenue by the same name, was built by King Amanullah in 1923 as the centrepiece of what was to be the brand spanking new capital city of Afghanistan.

Unfortunately, things didn't turn out as planned.

The imposing Palace, designed on French lines and set in French style gardens was never actually used for what it was intended, becoming firstly home to the Justice Ministry and then later, during the civil war, taken over by the legendary Ahmad Shah Massoud and used as headquarters for the Defence Ministry.

All that remains of this architectural folly now is a strangely haunted shell.

Yet another movie prop, perhaps one of those futuristic movies of survival following a nuclear holocaust.

It floated like a toy castle in the dust haze as we approached it, being repeatedly blotted out by the pea-soup atmosphere, growing, then shrinking in stature through some freakish meteorological trickery.

It could well have been a mirage.

The desolate, rubble-strewn expanse of flattened ministries, schools, villas, shops, off to the right of the avenue, once home to many of the city's elite now a camping ground for Kuchis and fat-tailed sheep, is already set for reconstruction, plots and boundaries marked out with rocks, bricks, barbed wire.

There is no sign of the famous Poplar trees which once lined this road only sparse grass, rubble and the anguished whispers of ghosts.

'Two foreigners were killed over there,' Sabir tells me pointing towards a huddle of low houses, high walls on our left. 'It just happened. Maybe two weeks ago.'

I recalled seeing something about the incident in the newspaper and hiding it from my husband in case it adversely influenced his decision to allow me to travel to Kabul alone.

'Two men,' Waliyat Khan continued. 'Heads bashed in with stones. Blood everywhere. Brains too. All over the garden. My cousin saw it,' he confirmed with grim satisfaction.

Sabir disputes the gruesome details.

Waliyat Khan rolls his eyes in mock horror, pulls at his beard, his ears.

'They were stupid men,' he narrates. 'From some Europe country pretending to be Afghan,' he spits out of the jeep window in disgust.

'They wore *shalwar kameez*, *pakol* hats and *chadars* but how can a Europe person be an Afghan. Beards too but not Afghan. They didn't even speak Pashto or Dari. Everybody in Kabul knew about them. They had no money, no manners and no honour. At first people treated them as guests. This is our custom. Our honour. But we soon came to know that they are not good people. They eat all the time with poor people. They sleep with poor people or on the road. Somehow they come out here. Maybe someone brings them, maybe they walk. Who knows.'

He shrugs his shoulders, confers with Sabir and Hamid, concludes with a flourish, 'So they go to live in garden of ruined house here and they get bottle of vodka or something like whiskey from somewhere and they make themselves party in middle of night. They shout for women and make big noise, big fool things. Someone goes out, nobody knows who someone is. One they smash head with stones, one they strangle like this,' he demonstrates, sticking his tongue out, gagging for breath, thrashing his arms in fair imitation. 'Then... fuuuuthhhh...they are finished off dead.'

We parked in the sparse shade of a clump of dusty Acacia trees where a guard was sound asleep on a flowered mattress. I jumped out and took his photograph much to the amusement of his fellow guard who strolled over from across the road to check us out.

The devastated palace loomed over us, vague outlines of flower beds, pathways, stumps of trees poking through rubble, sand and small stones.

Accompanied by Waliyat Khan and Sabir I walked up the sweeping driveway for a closer view, cameras at the ready.

The eerie stillness disturbed by the whistling wind and what I presumed to be a distant truck revving its protesting engine. Maybe it had got stuck, bogged down in the desert-like environment.

I had just positioned myself, focused the Nikon for what I hoped would be a good shot, when a pair of Afghan Army soldiers in full regalia marched like clockwork toys, old fashioned lead soldiers, out of a yawning palace portal and firmly told us, 'Taking photographs of Army installations is not allowed.'

I clicked then closed!

Wondering how on earth this totally demoralized heap of stones could be classified as an army installation.

The toy soldiers marched away in the direction from which we had come, we walked slowly on.

Darulaman Palace is built sideways on to the road, the main bulk of its construction, an 'E' without the central leg, faces in a completely different direction altogether, faces out over a rolling plain inhabited by a sprawling ISAF base, Canadian, I think.

An endless vision of hastily built barracks, tents, APCs and the other heavy 'machinery' of war, garrisoned by rolls and rolls of razor wire stretching as far as the eye could see, machine-gun emplacements manned and at the ready.

The palace on high ground, the sprawling camp below.

We had a bird's eye-view.

It looked like a prison camp to be honest.

It felt uncomfortable.

Intimidating.

I turned my back on the out of place invaders feeling unseen eyes penetrating the very core of my being.

Concentrating on the palace again, trying to place the direction in which the sound of heavy machinery was coming from, it wasn't from the army base but the source was somewhere near at hand and growling louder.

Spotting the partial remains of a highly decorated, upper floor room, the outer wall blown away, removing itself like the front of a dolls house, exposing painted, moulded ceilings, smashed furniture, a broken wall mirror, I considered, briefly, sneaking a quick photograph or two but...if I did, if I was caught, then my companions, as well as myself, would have a very rough time of it indeed. My cameras went back beneath my *chadar*.

It was only then that I noticed the razor wire concertina blocking access to the large, central courtyard, green camouflage netting above sandbags on the gaping second floor, an observation camera, a machine-gun, a pair of sunglasses, a hat.

The Afghan Army was well and truly in residence, palace guards in position years too late, an anachronism.

'They are watching ISAF who are watching them watch us,' said Waliyat Khan with a sheepish grin. 'Let's go. I don't like this place.'

Sabir, in cheeky boy fashion, idiotically jumped up and down on the spot waving his arms in the air to attract attention.

'Lunatic,' cursed Waliyat Khan kicking him soundly on the behind with a force that should have knocked Sabir completely off his feet but didn't. 'Come on. Let's go.'

As we performed an abrupt about turn, I suddenly realized that the sound of heavy machinery wasn't that at all.

The Parwan Wind was howling through the palace.

It was swinging, grinding, clattering every movable bit of the almost skeletal framework left standing.

The sound set my teeth on edge.

Raised my hackles.

Goosebumps.

The building was shrieking its intense agony.

It was downright unnerving.

We all heaved a collective sigh of relief as we drove away.

My hopes of visiting the adjacent, under-repair Museum put firmly on the back-burner.

Much better to get away from here.

Fast.

– VIII –

A serious debate and it was decided that we better eat something before heading off to a place called Kargha. 'Beautiful place with plenty of water,' Sabir said. 'Much enjoyment place.'

I hoped that it wasn't another zoo!

We stopped at a Hazara *kebab* joint where we were served a dozen skewers of mutton *kebab*, including chunks of fat, salad and a huge *nan* each for the equivalent of 50 rupees, a feast for which even Hamid joined us.

Waliyat Khan studiously removed all the fat from his skewers.

'Hey!' I said to his astonishment. 'That's the best bit!'

'Cholesterol,' he justified pulling himself up straight in indignation. 'You shouldn't eat it either.'

Heading out of Kabul on the Kandahar road we ground to a sudden halt in the centre of a large, extremely busy bazaar.

Hamid actually smiled as he disappeared off into the throng with Waliyat Khan in tow.

'Something for Pickernicker,' Sabir told me.

They returned a brief few minutes later with the biggest watermelon I had set eyes on in ages and off we went again.

The city suburbs are under construction.

'Bungalows' resembling those in Karachi, Defence Phase-V in amongst bombed out ruins and mud bricks houses.

Money is certainly pouring in from somewhere.

A small band of Kuchis…down to three mangy-looking camels.

'All gone soon,' observed Waliyat Khan dryly.

Branching off the main drag and heading for the hills.

The tops of chimneys and roofs, the tops of orchards behind high mud walls.

It was then that I noticed Hamid gripping a huge, wicked looking knife in the hand he was changing gear with.

I asked if he was expecting bandits.

He smiled and cracked a joke in Dari which I didn't understand.

Almost crying with laughter at the unexpected joke, Waliyat Khan assured me, 'No bandits. No problem. I hope.'

Why the knife then?

The road, well surfaced but narrow, meandered between fields where people were tending to their crops, their goats.

We passed a large, tented UNHCR school, caught a glimpse of chairs and blackboards through open flaps.

Unfortunately, it was already closed for the day.

I would have loved to learn more about it and the educational programme it was running.

Kabul Golf Club materialized on our right.

Overgrown greens and seemingly empty buildings.

Closed but reopening soon, I was told.

I couldn't help wondering what might happen if you did get a hole in one!

I wanted to stop and photograph a beautiful patch of blue flowering Solanum, over a ditch and off to the left of the road.

'No,' I was immediately and forcefully told.

'Mines.'

How could this have escaped my memory even for a second?

'Only walk or drive where someone else has gone before you,' stressed Sabir. 'In the city, in the countryside, everyplace in Afghanistan. Mines, bombs everywhere. Very dangerous. Maybe just one foot step off the road and bang. All dead. Even if vehicle breaks down then no going off road. Too many go bang.'

Jolted back to reality, I immediately removed the rose-tinted glasses which had slipped into place.

The picturesque, greenly rolling countryside, the wind-stirred pine forests, distant blue mountains all contain instant death.

A sobering truth indeed.

Immediately behind the golf course a series of very high, very narrow, not quite terraces, grassy walled in amongst blue stones, gave me a broad hint at what to expect. A parapet, a road across the top of this man-made incline and yes, a dam, a lake with an unparalleled view of the distant, snow-capped, Paghman mountains.

An unexpected paradise.

Kargha Dam and Lake, constructed during the late 1950s and early 1960s, the slate blue waters, much shrunk in size now due to the long lasting and terrible drought which has added to the people's misery. Brought to their knees by decades of war, the drought was the last straw for many. People who had managed to hang on, eke out a living between fighting, couldn't find the strength to cope with a searing drought.

No water.

No life.

Orchards which had survived the scorched earth policy of the Soviet Union, livestock, already much reduced in number by the depredations of all sides, right or wrong, invaders and patriots, shrivelled, died on their feet under the cruel onslaught of a natural catastrophe.

'The water used to be up to here,' said Sabir, pointing to a spot at least a hundred feet away from the current shore. 'Not enough rain, not enough snow but it is still enjoyment place.'

The rusting hulk of a Soviet tank perched precariously on top of one of the surrounding hills.

A metal tombstone to history.

A chilling reminder of what may, quite possibly, happen again.

The breezy atmosphere was redolent with the perfume of wild roses, the scent of Juniper trees and something else, that I couldn't identify, drifting towards us across the softly undulating plains from the hazy blue-and-white peaks far ahead.

Distance reduced tents dotted one area of the tussocky plains.

More nomads.

An endangered breed.

I imagined them as Michener described in his *Caravans* but know that today's truth is different.

There is no longer any room for 'romance' in their world, and I doubt if there ever was.

Survival is the name of the game and for the Kuchis time appears to be running out fast.

The drought spells yet another vicious nail in the coffin of their freedom.

'Many people come here for pickernicker,' Waliyat Khan tells me, breaking my river of thought. 'On weekend, on holiday. Look,' he points enthusiastically towards a distant shore. 'Boat trips. We will all go on a boat trip.'

The three musketeers are back in action, smiles of delighted anticipation dispelling any overtures of gloom.

'No thanks. No boats,' I disappoint them though it may have been nice.

I just wasn't in the mood.

'Restaurant soon. We have pickernicker,' says Sabir, not put out in the least.

Then, rounding a corner beneath pine trees and clambering roses, it is my turn to shout 'Stop'.

Wonder of wonders…a large greenhouse.

DUST MOTES – 11

'I have looked after this precious greenhouse and garden for more than thirty years,' Kaka Azhar proudly tells me once he has agreed to show us around.

He wasn't too happy at the intrusion initially, weathered face, lined and scored beneath his grubby cap, screwing up in concentration whilst he debated with himself whether to allow us into his territory at all.

I complemented him on some beautiful pots of geraniums and this seemed to do the trick.

'Up here was a lot of fighting,' he told me shaking his aged head at the terrible memories. 'Russians, *Mujahideen*, *Taliban*, everyone came to fight here. Many bad people, a few good ones too. Tanks, planes, rockets, bombs, much shooting, much destruction. This greenhouse', he gestured towards it with a gnarled, work-worn hand, 'broken many times. My plants killed by the cold as I couldn't find glass to fix it. First time I fixed it with wood. Next time with tin. Next time, no wood and no tin. Next time cardboard. Next time no cardboard only old cloth. Then next time and next time and next time nothing to fix it with, so during snow time plants died. I light the fire but the plants still died.'

He is still wary of my questions but I manage, eventually, to learn that he had been with the *Mujahideen* at various points, fighting locally and being badly injured at some point.

'Only one brother left now,' he says grimly. 'Everyone else martyred. Too much killing, too much fighting.'

Inside his treasured greenhouse, I was amazed to see that the floor is constructed out of natural stones, crazy paving without cracks.

The back wall of this large structure is also of stone, each block precisely cut and fitted.

Stone built seats surround a large fireplace set into this wall.

This is more than a greenhouse.

It is a livable work of art.

The roof is still made of plywood, restricting the light to a certain degree.

'Glass for the walls I finally managed to find two years ago,' he continues. 'Now I try to get for the roof. Try to make everything as it was before the wars came and spoilt everything. Spoilt the life for the people, spoilt my country, broke my greenhouse.'

A double peach coloured geranium catches my eye.

Rummaging in my capricious shoulder bag I extract a packet of mixed flower seeds and offer to exchange this for a geranium cutting.

He stares at me in horror.

'These are not my plants,' he tells me quite angrily. 'These are the plants of my employer. No cuttings.'

He starts to shout.

I apologize but he shouts louder.

He starts to push Waliyat Khan who pushes back.

It seems that a fight is brewing.

'Please take the seeds anyway,' I insist, holding the packet out to him at arms length.

He shakes his head stubbornly looking at the packet with the gravest suspicion.

'Yes. Take it,' says Waliyat Khan, Sabir has already retreated towards the jeep.

'No geranium,' he shouts again, waving a finger in my face.

'No more questions. Go now. Go away.'

Snatching the seed packet he gestures towards the open door, pulling himself up to his full height, glaring ferociously.

'Broken,' he shouts. 'Everything is broken'.

'Sick in here,' says Waliyat Khan sadly, pointing towards his head. 'All the fighting did this.'

– IX –

An under-renovation restaurant, another Aga Khan Trust for Culture project, on the lake shores with yet another delightful garden in which two gnarled, ancient Wisteria vines attract my attention. The two attendant *malis* insist that the wisterias have yellow and brown blossoms which I find hard to believe as such colours are not in this species palette. A magnificent, purple leaved plum tree which bears matching purple fruit, huge grape vines, fantastic roses with perfume to match, a view across the shrunken lake to the plain which rolls in unbroken waves to touch the feet of the distant Paghman mountains.

'See those small trees over there,' says Waliyat Khan gesturing to a large, walled enclosure on the opposite shore. 'That is an orchard. That land belongs to Mr Jekdalek. He is going to build a house there. No house yet. Trees first. House next.'

An idyllic spot to live and yet another side to Anwar that I hadn't previously encountered.

The man has become a mystery to me.

A mystery I hope to unravel when I can finally pin him down.

'Pickernicker now,' insist Sabir in the grating tone of a spoilt child.

'Pickernicker next to water.'

Hamid arrives carrying the watermelon from the jeep, knife at the ready.

This is what the knife was for.

For the watermelon not bandits!

One more surprise in store.

A visit to the *Mehman khana* of someone by the name of Mullah Ezzat I believe.

Two houses in a lakeside compound, prime real estate I would guess and one more beautiful garden.

Grapes in full bloom, rose arbours, water wheels in naturally designed channels, even a most impressive swimming pool full of limpid green water and fallen rose petals.

We sat, sipping green tea and eating sweets wrapped in gold foil, in the shade of a huge *chinar* tree whose leaves, rustled by a refreshing cool breeze, almost lulled me to sleep.

I could have remained in that timeless garden for ever but...time to head back to the dusty city, getting mixed up with a seemingly endless convoy of ISAF troops and their lethal machinery on the way.

They really give me the creeps.

Thundering along the narrow, countryside road at breakneck speed.

Spewing dust and exhaust fumes.

Exuding tension.

Hamid pulled over to one side and let them go.

'Continental Hotel now,' announced Sabir.

'No thanks,' I told him much to his intense disappointment.

'Why not?' he demanded.

'It's just a big hotel,' I explained. 'I've seen enough big hotels in other places. They are all the same. Anyway, we are already late in getting back and I need to find a PCO to phone my husband first.'

'Telephone in hotel,' he announced with satisfaction.

'Too expensive,' I retorted, deflating his ego.

Phone call made, knife returned to the watermelon vendor, we finally made it back to the villa where Farhad was pacing the driveway.

'We're only a little late,' I apologized. 'About an hour. Sorry about this.'

'That's okay Banafsha it's just that I need to go and find Anwar. He's with Fahim somewhere or other and I can't get him on the phone. I have an urgent message for him so better go. See you later.'

Fahim, better known as General Fahim, former military leader of the Northern Alliance, now Defence Minister and a person to be reckoned with. What was cooking now?

He was back in under an hour, rushing in for a shower and change of clothes.

'Anwar is just coming over, Banafsha,' he told me triumphantly after answering a very short phone call whilst polishing his shoes.

'He won't be able to stay long though. Just wants to say hello. He's trying to arrange an interview with Karzai for you in the next day or two.'

He rushes off, recklessly throwing Telabaz's car through its paces as he zooms out of the gate and into the heavy evening traffic.

Fifteen minutes later he's back again.

'Sorry Banafsha,' he grimaces ruefully. 'Anwar can't make it right now. He'll see you tomorrow. He promises. Got to go and find him again now. See you later.'

Farhad the yo-yo!

'Naeem has put too much salt in the *lobia*,' Waliyat Khan comes to inform me. 'Do you like *bhindi aloo*?'

'Yes,' I tell him. 'Very much.'

'I'll just go to the bazaar and get some then. Will you be alright here?'

'No problem Waliyat Khan. No problem at all.'

Drooping with exhaustion on my mattress seat-cum-bed, I drink another cup of coffee, swallow another antihistamine and hope for the best.

My sinus is agony.

The dust is taking its toll.

The yo-yo rushes in again.

'Completely forgot to tell you that a guy is arriving from Mazar-i-Sharif. He lives in London but is doing some stuff here right now. He's a nice guy Banafsha. Speaks good English. He's having the room across the hallway so don't be afraid when he comes in.'

Farhad departs once more and Waliyat Khan comes in with supper.

I thought he had gone to buy it from the bazaar but he only went for the ingredients then cooked it himself.

He only cooks for *rishtadars*, he proudly claims as he lays the feast before me with a flourish.

'Guest arriving from Mazar-i-Sharif in night. No problem. Lock your door when I go out.'

He goes.

I firmly bolt the door.

Sit with my thoughts for company until sleep catches me unaware.

Shots in the night.

The rumble of heavy transport outside the gate.

The whoosh of a rocket fired close by.

An echoing thud…also close by.

I hear Farhad and his girl come in.

He whispering, her giggling.

No guest arrives.

END OF PART FOUR

PART FIVE

– I –

Bleary eyed as usual each morning, Farhad surfaced, furiously scratching his chin as he came to tell me, 'Anwar has just phoned. His driver is off somewhere so I am just going to pick him up and bring him here.'

Finally!

His girl came to introduce herself to me whilst Farhad went out to dust off the car.

A pointless exercise, the wind is blowing stronger than ever.

DUST MOTES – 12

Squeezed into and bulging out of denim jeans, embroidered flowers on the wide bottoms, a plunge neck, skin tight T-shirt which didn't leave much to the imagination, revealing a thick roll of flab around her non-existent waist, she slid into the room on tiptoe, barefoot, waving her hands around and blowing on her newly painted, luminous pink nails.

'Hi!' she smiled. 'I want to invite you to come with me to a love wedding at 5 p.m. this afternoon. It is a real love wedding. Not arranged. It is wonderful. Just like me and Farhad. We are going to have a love wedding too. You must come.'

As there didn't appear to be anything else on my agenda I agreed, with reservations as I normally avoid weddings like the plague.

'I will pick you up at 5 p.m.,' she continued. 'My mother and one of my sisters will come too. I am going to wear Punjabi dress which I bought when Farhad took me to Murree during the snow time. We didn't know you were there or we would have visited but we are going back on honeymoon so will visit then.'

In her early twenties, Farhad's girl, who I have decided not to name for reasons of my own, is of medium height, her twinkling brown eyes full of mischief under a bushy thatch of brown hair.

She doesn't look like an Afghan to me.

More like a Russian.

A *babushka*.

Big boned.

Built like a tank, a female wrestler.

'My mother took all of her children to Peshawar during the Russian time,' she told me.

'My father has a good job so he stayed here but we all left. I went to school in Peshawar and then trained as a midwife but I am not doing any work now. Just looking after Farhad. Then we will get married and I will spend all my time looking after him.'

'When are you getting married?' I asked.

'Very soon. Maybe next month,' she said rather uncertainly.

'We will live in this house and be very happy.'

'When did you come back to Afghanistan,' I enquired, thinking that somehow her wedding plans had an unreal feel to them.

She wanted to believe what she was telling me but...it didn't ring true.

'We came after *Taliban* had gone but it was better in Peshawar. I really had a good time there. Here it is difficult. All the time in the house until I met Farhad. Now I come here but we have to be very careful. It will be different when we are married.'

She seemed a good hearted soul, obviously infatuated with Farhad but...

'Do you like my *abaya*?' she wanted to know carefully displaying the embroidered edges of the black silk robe draped across her broad shoulders. 'We got it in Dubai when Farhad took me there and a headscarf to match.'

An unmarried Afghan girl holidaying with her boyfriend in Murree and Dubai.

Most unusual.

'What do your parents think of you coming here, staying here before marriage?'

'At first they don't like it but now...' She shrugged her shoulders, giggling like a naughty school girl. 'We had engagement. Everybody knows this. Marriage will be soon,' she dismisses the subject with a wave of one taloned hand, flashing her small engagement ring as proof of the situation.

'You will come to the love wedding today?'

'Is it really at 5 p.m.?' This sounds a strange time for a wedding to me. 'How long will it last.'

'Only two, maybe three hours at the most. Not late. These things are not late in Kabul. I will come for you at 5 p.m. I have to go now. Farhad will take me home before he picks up Mr Jekdalek. Mr Jekdalek doesn't know that I come here or he would be very angry.'

Not know!

Who does she think she's kidding!!!

Waliyat Khan knows, Naeem knows, everyone who comes and goes knows, certainly Anwar knows but I keep quiet on this.

Swathed in black, head down against the wind, she rushes out, climbs into the front of the car and they roar off into the morning traffic.

– II –

Two hours later there is still no sign of Farhad or Anwar.

I sit sipping coffee, waiting as usual.

A car eventually arrives.

Farhad, alone.

'Sorry Banafsha,' he grins wryly 'Anwar is too busy to come right now but he is sending someone to take you to the Stadium so that you can interview the girl athletes you asked about.'

Two girls heading for the Athens Olympics, interviews I couldn't let pass me by.

'The car will be here any minute so you better be ready and would you mind moving rooms? You can have the one with the TV. Some guests are coming tonight so this room is needed. You don't mind do you?'

What could I say?

'Oh Banafsha,' he threw in as he was leaving. 'Anwar is still trying to arrange an interview with Karzai for you. He should know later today.' Then he is gone, again.

Naeem tells me, 'Twenty, maybe thirty big men coming for dinner.'

Obviously I am expected to be invisible if they are still here when I get back from the wedding.

I wash my face, brush my hair and emerge from the bathroom to find Anwar standing in the hallway peering around the door to my room.

A dapper man in sand coloured slacks, pastel check shirt, sand coloured suede jacket, everything reeking designer label expensive.

He puts out a hand, kisses the air on both sides of my flustered face.

He has caught me on the hop.

These actions are completely new to me.

I see nothing of the former *Mujahideen* commander I once knew in this sudden stranger.

'I am a bad host,' he apologizes.

I agree.

'Someone is coming to take you to the Stadium now. A man is coming here for a meeting with me. Are you ready to go?'

'Yes,' I tell him, feeling very much in the way. 'When will you have time to be interviewed?'

'You want interview with me?' he sounds surprised.

'Yes Anwar. I have lots of things to ask you.'

'Okay. I will come for two hours on Saturday,' he promises.

He is a very busy man indeed.

'Before I leave Anwar, there are a couple of things I want to give you.' I already have my doubts about him turning up on Saturday.

I dig out the hand embroidered *chadar* for his mother, my mother, and a handful of seed packets, flowers for his garden. I couldn't think what else to bring for him and the seeds seemed like a good idea.

He is delighted, smiles broadly, displaying an array of badly filled teeth, a grey metal grin which somehow menaces.

A fat man, a balloon encased in a shiny black suit, waddles in through the front door on astonishingly small feet.

Anwar points him towards the TV room.

'Some guests are coming,' he starts to tell me.

'Farhad said.' I cut him off as Waliyat Khan shouts that my driver has come.

'Saturday,' promises Anwar as I depart to find an entire bus plus driver and guard at my disposal.

Everything seems to be ridiculous.

– III –

A different bus.

A different time.

Travelling to war on the front seat of a hired coach, which trailed tinsel ribbons, and bells from fenders and roof rack, with the added unreality of paintings and fancy metal work on every square inch of bodywork, I contemplated the boxes of mines pushed under my seat, the hand grenades in the luggage rack, the guns and the twenty-four desperadoes sitting behind me, and told myself, 'It'll be okay, you're a woman now with four bodyguards to boot!'

'You die before she dies,' they were told.

That was then.

This was now.

The bus antiseptic, white, shining, undecorated except for the logo of the Olympic Committee of Afghanistan.

The driver and guard both uniformed.

I wrapped tightly in a *chadar*.

Only this was the same.

I look out of the windows as Kabul flashes by.

An uninterrupted stream of conflicting images.

The women of Afghanistan have long been portrayed as repressed, and upon arrival I had expected to see nothing more of them than shadowy, *burkha* clad figures darting furtively in and out of ruined buildings.

Wrong.

Instead I am stunned to see young women wearing long skirts, fashionably slit to the knee, exposing white *shalwars* or, for the more daring, 1950s style fishnet stockings.

The skirts are topped by loose blouses, piled up hair draped with soft headscarves flowing in the breeze.

Others wear bell-bottomed trousers or jeans and jackets.

All stride confidently along, bundles of books under their arms, past completely renovated buildings or buildings which have not suffered any war damage at all.

The women, in Kabul at least, are thriving, working in all walks of life and moving towards what is, hopefully, a wonderful future, although this could change, explode, at any second.

Absolutely nothing is certain here.

Nothing that is except for the fact that this city, the people in it, appear on a different movie screen than the one I had naively watched inside my head prior to my arrival.

The Afghanistan of Jegdalek times, with the very limited vision this allowed me, was more like the North West Frontier Province of Pakistan, the people who inhabited it the same.

Tribal.

Earthy.

Tough.

Kabul though, and the people who 'own' it are totally different.

One could easily mistake them for inhabitants of the former Soviet Union, the former aggressors, the former occupying power.

These are Central Europeans not the Pathans of my previous experience.

City people not mountain ones.

'Kabuli Pathans,' a derogatory term often used in Pakistan, takes on a new meaning.

This revelation comes as a shock.

Reaching the Stadium, I am escorted up the stairs, along corridors to a room humming with activity.

Obviously an office, it is occupied by a number of men and women hovering, laughing and joking over computers and masses of associated paperwork.

'This is Madame Shamsul Hayat,' a middle-aged man with a smarmy attitude informs me as an elderly lady steps forward to take my hand. 'She has been responsible for the female athletes for the past two years.'

The smiling duenna, iron-grey hair piled in a high bun with a Spanish, black lace mantilla artfully arranged over the top, indicates that I should sit on a low, brown, plastic covered chair next to a huge fridge from which she promptly takes out an ice cold bottle of Pepsi which I don't want.

Another lady, taller, vivacious, immaculate, heavy make up, shining black hair drawn back and fastened at the nape of her neck by a huge, multi-coloured plastic grip, forces me to accept the refreshment, chattering away to me in non-stop Dari. It is 'Banafsha Jan' this and 'Banafsha Jan' that. I don't have a clue what she is talking about.

'She is the Deputy Director of Finance.' Mr Ingratiatingly Smarmy informs me as he pulls up a chair close, too close, by my side. I don't like him at all. He has reptilian eyes, a darting, pointed tongue. A snake.

'I will translate for you with the athletes.'

Thankfully, as it turns out, I don't need him but, he doesn't move away.

Dust Motes – 13

Extremely nervous, chewing on her non-existent finger nails, Friba Rezzai, enters the busy room struggling hard to conceal her apprehension and failing miserably.

She is 17 years old and going for gold.

Leaving first for Turkey and then on to the Athens Olympics the following morning.

She perches on a chair opposite mine, carefully arranging the folds of a brilliant turquoise, green and gold *shalwar kameez*, purchased recently in India and now worn 'for luck' and waits for the interview to begin.

I try to put her at ease, make her smile.

It works.

In softly accented English she tells me, 'I am very happy and nervous to go to Athens. This is a big opportunity for the Afghan people. Now that we have peace we have this opportunity. This is the first group of Afghan athletes to go to the Olympic Games after peace has come. This is good for Afghanistan and especially good for girls.'

Born in Sar-i-Pul, Jowzjan province, in the north of the country, Friba, a member of the Hazara community, fled, along with the rest of her family, to Peshawar when she was only 8 years old, returning to Afghanistan two years ago. She is one of the lucky ones as many of the Hazara Shia community from the same area took refuge in Mazar-i-Sharif in neighbouring Balkh province and it was people from this community who gave the *Taliban* their first ever military set back, driving them out of this historic city in 1997. The *Taliban* came back though and were victorious the second time around, viciously massacring approximately 6,000 Hazara Shias there in a grim form of retribution.

'In Peshawar there was no opportunity for me to do sports,' Friba continues, sipping at my unwanted drink.

'I was always studying.'

On returning to Kabul she quickly joined a club and began, of all things, training to be a boxer.

'I know that boxing is an unusual sport for girls, but I wanted to do competitions like Mike Tyson, like Laila Ali,' she explained punching the air with her fists to demonstrate, her shyness evaporating in the process.

After four months of boxing training her coach advised that her weight was more appropriate for judo.

'On this advice I switched over to judo and now have a brown belt. I attend school in the morning and come here for training afterwards. I also do weights. I was in a judo competition in India a few months ago but didn't take any top position. Now, whilst I am very excited about the Olympics I am very nervous as to whether I will win. I worry about this a lot because our training is not as good as in other countries, though we do have a good Norwegian coach. Belonging to the Hazara community has posed some problems in my life, it is difficult for people from our community so we have to fight but my parents, four brothers and three sisters are all very proud of me. They are happy that I am representing my country and my community in the Olympics.'

Friba also has other plans mapped out.

'After I finish school I want to be a lawyer specializing in women's rights. Afghanistan needs women's rights. This is what I intend to do. The Olympics is the first big step in my life and this will be the next.'

DUST MOTES – 14

Dressed in black trousers and matching jacket with a gauzy, grey *dupatta* flung carelessly over her head, Rubina Mqueir, elbows her way into the room with all the arrogance she can muster.

Seventeen with the world at her feet or so she seems to expect.

Taller and far more confident than the diminutive Friba, Rubina only began her athletics career a mere eight months ago and competes in the 100m sprint.

'Running makes me feel so free,' she enthuses. 'It was my own decision to take up this sport.'

Her family is originally from Kunduz and took refuge in Pakistan where she was born.

'We came back to Afghanistan thirteen years ago when I was four years old,' she explained.

Living in Kabul through the years of the *Taliban* occupation Rubina only has bad memories of that time and is understandably reluctant to talk about it.

'Just sitting around at home, no studies, nothing,' is all she will say. 'We are not allowed to talk about the political situation,' she adds, putting me firmly in my place.

Rubina has already competed in sporting events in Iran where she obtained fifth place, and more recently, the SAF games in Pakistan where she came sixth.

'If it becomes necessary for me to stop running then I intend to become a doctor, specializing in orthopaedics, so that I can continue to be associated with athletes,' she tells me quite firmly.

She has written her life in advance.

There is no room for compromise, of any sort, in her iron-clad attitude.

(Interviews with Friba and Rubina first appeared in *'The Review'*, *Dawn* in the edition 1–7 July 2004).

Dust Motes – 15

Mr Ingratiatingly Smarmy refuses to let me leave the room until he has also had his say.

'I fled to Quetta when the *Mujahideen* entered Kabul in 1992,' he self-importantly informs me without being asked.

'I stayed there through the *Taliban* years and came back fourteen months ago. I am forty years old with a wife and three children. Things are very difficult for me here.'

'I trained in TV montage, editing and camera in Czechoslovakia and am fluent in Pashto, Dari, Urdu, Russian and English.'

He is slightly balding, light brown haired, has protruding blue-grey eyes and would pass for a Russian any day of the week. His baggy, very shiny, grey suit with overlarge, cloth-covered buttons, adds to this impression.

'I have to work here and also at Kabul television station as it is necessary to have at least two jobs in order to try to survive economically speaking. The television station is run by *Mujahideen*,' he spits the word '*Mujahideen*' out with bitterness and loathing. 'These *Mujahideen* know nothing about the television business. They should not be there.'

He feels extremely let down, angry at life in general, both past and present.

'I couldn't get proper work in Pakistan because I was a refugee so was forced to work as a cook in a private house for a while.'

I try to picture him slaving over a hot stove, doing the dishes, serving food.

No picture materializes.

I certainly wouldn't trust someone like this in my kitchen.

'I only earn 2,000 Afghanis per month here and something else at the television station but the rent of an apartment is at least 5,000 Afghanis per month so my family can only have one small room in an apartment that we have to share with relatives. During the Soviet time I had a good job, a beautiful place to live and now I am reduced to this.'

He complains that the electricity supply is unreliable, that the water has to be boiled or purchased and that he needs more money to buy Pepsi for his children and a generator so that they can still watch television when the power goes.

Then his children also need a variety of other things such as brand name jeans, joggers, named bicycles which I've never heard of.

They must have these things so that they don't get 'an inferiority complex.'

Which planet does this guy inhabit?

He wants things that most people in this part of the world, including me, don't have.

'How can I even work properly when there are four other people working in the same room,' he whines on gesticulating around the office which is not small, is resplendent with a fridge, fans and computers.

'All the people in positions, they are all *Mujahideen* and ministers, just put all of the aid money in their pockets and nothing filters down to the people.'

He means himself.

I wonder at the evidence of my own eyes.

There is electricity, running water, sewage and road systems, schools and colleges have reopened, new buildings, commercial and residential are going up at the speed of light. There are parks, gardens, sports grounds.

There is corruption, no doubt about it, it happens everywhere at some level or other but there is also progress.

'Can you help me to get a good job, maybe in television, in Pakistan?' he has the audacity to ask.

I really don't think we want him or anyone else of this ilk.

'I am held back here because of my Czech training and because I speak Russian.'

This could well be true.

'If I speak out then I am called a communist.'

He appears more of a capitalist in my opinion.

'I just have to get out of this country,' he insists. 'I do not belong here any more.'

I wonder if he ever did.

– IV –

Back at 'home' the lawn, the boundary walls, the driveway, an array of plastic tables and chairs have been hosed down twice as far as I know.

Carpets have been laid on part of the lawn, driveway and completely cover the patio and house entrance.

'Elephants foot' all over the place.

Now the lawn is getting watered again.

'To keep down the dust,' says Farhad.

Apparently his girl and her sisters are busy cooking for the mysterious guests and will bring the food over later.

Whoops!

So much for my room.

I just had to shift to the TV room as all of the mattresses and pillows are being taken out and arranged around the carpets on the patio along with even more cushions commandeered from the guardhouse.

Now they are taking the mattresses and pillows out of here too.

All that is left is the very hard, single bed which looks like it came from a western mail order catalogue.

This is going to be some session it seems.

At least I do have the bed in here but don't know how I'll sleep, let alone get back in to the compound after the *shadi* and how on earth will I manage to go to the loo!

This place will be high risk and high security tonight.

I would much rather stay, be a fly on the wall, than go to the *shadi* but Farhad won't hear of it.

I'm a journalist, it sounds as if the entire Cabinet will be feasting here.

I want to interview them all.

Watch them in action.

Listen to what they have to say.

See them perform.

'It is not a place for you to be Banafsha,' Farhad insists.

'If you don't want to go to the *shadi* then you can go someplace else. You can't stay here.'

5 p.m. comes and goes…naturally…no sign of anyone to take me to the damned wedding.

I have just learnt that Zalmay Khalilzed, the American Afghan Ambassador has invited himself to the party, and as he travels with at least fifteen bodyguards this will put a strain on the food, so Farhad's girl is still cooking.

I want to stay here more than ever.

'No Banafsha,' says Farhad quite sharply. He is getting fed up of me I can tell.

'I will take you over to my fiancé's house right now.'

He does.

No further argument permitted.

The house is in a mud walled compound directly opposite a huge American base.

Its occupants hiding behind barricades, razor wire, concrete filled drums at intervals across the road, manned machine-gun towers, sandbags and huge signs that warn, in Dari and English, 'LETHAL ACTION MAY BE TAKEN AGAINST YOU IF YOU ACT SUSPICIOUSLY OR TAKE PHOTOGRAPHS.' I note the use of 'Lethal' and put my cameras away... again.

Farhad's girl emerged briefly from the kitchen, sweat running in rivulets down her flushed face.

She looked fatter and more hassled than ever and was up to her eyes in mountains of freshly cooked *mantu*, *ashak* and platters of salad with more on the way.

'I won't be long,' she says giving me a wet hug. 'I just want to show you my Punjabi outfit. The one I am going to wear to the *shadi*.'

Luminous royal blue synthetic fabric emblazoned with lots and lots of gold thread embroidery.

It looks rather small for her ample figure and I can't imagine how on earth she will manage to squeeze herself into it without bursting the seams.

She introduces me to her mother, a shrewdly calculating rotund woman in a silver and black lurex skirt suit, lace edged, wide, white cotton *shalwar*, black plastic, square toed high heels, her grey hair in a long plait decorated with diamante edged black satin bows.

All dressed up and raring to go.

Another daughter, a pretty fifteen year old called Memoona, with hennaed hair tastefully tied back with a black ribbon, wearing an incredibly elegant, full length, black chiffon and black sequined tube, cut daringly low to expose a quite obvious cleavage was also ready to party. Her outfit completed by black plastic wedgies of huge proportions, multi-coloured glitter all over their base, German silver bracelets on both wrists and dangerous looking thumb rings on both hands.

Memoona introduces me to her father, a small, tired man in a crumpled grey *shalwar kameez*, with a grey beard and orange hennaed hair who has been, and still is, a foreign currency dealer in the same bank for over thirty-eight years. He has been here through whatever the wars have thrown at him. He is a survivor.

He has two wives and fifteen children all living in this *haveli* which stinks of open gutters, is full of rats, flies, mosquitoes and noise.

'We used to sleep on the roof in hot weather,' he tells me. 'But since the base was built across the road we can't go up there anymore or they might shoot us.'

'You must come and stay here,' he invites me. 'It must be very lonely for you at Farhad's house. You will be happier here with all of my family to keep you company. It would be better.'

I try to explain that I enjoy being alone, need the peace and quiet in order to work.

He does not understand.

This concept is completely alien to him, to all of them.

Farhad comes back from the kitchen where he has been sampling the food.

'I need to rush back now Banafsha. Lots of things still to do. You will go to the *shadi* with my fiancé's mother and Memoona.

'My fiancé will follow on in an hour or so when she has finished cooking. One of her brothers will drive.'

The two women disappear inside long black buttoned up coats, black headscarves, fade into the evening light.

They become anonymous, insubstantial shadows.

My red, flower patterned, full chemise, matching *shalwar* and white *chadar* were not an appropriate selection.

I feel like a lighthouse.

Our driver, we are in Telabaz's car which Farhad has left behind, looks and acts completely insane.

He drives far too fast.

I have read about the abnormally high rate of car accidents in Kabul so ask him to slow down.

He does.

For all of five minutes then speeds up again.

It seems like an awfully long way to the wedding venue.

We pass through areas where tiny mud houses cling to miniature mountain sides.

Shale slopes sprouting humanity.

They are piled up on top of each other, not an inch of space in between.

A '*desi*' Lego land.

People clamber up and down ladders from roof top to roof top.

A woman carries a goat in her arms.

Another a basket piled high with steaming *nan*.

Children leap antelope-like through the wavering shadows escaping from partly covered windows, from curtain hung doorways.

A mediaeval scene in modern times.

Yet another face of multidimensioned Kabul.

I suddenly realize that I have yet to see, or hear, a dog.

The *Taliban* banned people from keeping dogs but even wild ones are not around.

Most unusual for a Central Asian, even Asian, city.

Our meandering drive, backwards and forwards in time, takes us down the Kandahar road, through lamp light bazaars offering sizzling skewers of *kebabs*, dazzling pots of geraniums, piles of green onions, sacks of cement, plastic chandeliers, to an under construction maze right on the outskirts of the city.

A large marriage hall above a row of brand new shops.

No flashing fairy lights as in Pakistan.

No lights from the windows either as they were completely blacked out by heavy curtains.

All there was to indicate that we had arrived was noise.

Ear-splitting, head-aching noise.

I had already had enough.

– V –

A set of exceedingly white teeth glimmered fixedly out of the gloom, a hand-painted advertisement for a Chinese dentist, then floated in our direction.

The teeth belonged to our host for the event.

A late middle-aged doctor, dyed black hair surrounding a monks tonsure, heavy black moustache in a precise oblong which ended an inch or two either side of his pointed nose.

A glued on caterpillar.

A funeral black 1950s suit, spiv shoes, a badly stained, emerald green tie about six inches wide completed the strange ensemble.

He grinned in welcome.

He couldn't actually do otherwise, his teeth were far too big and it was impossible for him to close his mouth.

His features must totally collapse when he takes them out.

'Welcome, welcome,' he greets us not blinking an eye at my unexpected, or is it, presence.

He ushers us through a narrow doorway next to a brightly lighted pharmacy which is doing a roaring trade in plastic hair fasteners in the most eye-catching colours imaginable.

In semi-darkness, a wide, carpeted stairs leads up to the marriage venue.

The stairs are packed solid by women and girls of all ages stripping off their enveloping outdoor clothing, a few blue *burqas* included.

Half way up the stairs everyone grinds to a halt, preening themselves in the full length mirrored walls which someone had located in exactly the right place.

They stuff their discarded shrouds into plastic carrier bags chattering cattily away about who is wearing what.

I simply stand and stare.

I can't believe my eyes.

Madhuri Dixit to Scarlett O'Hara!

The doctor's daughters, six of them aged nine to twenty-two, all avid fans of 'Titanic' are each dressed in their own interpretation of their heroines high couture. Slim-fitting, floor-length, short-sleeved, low-neck dresses; royal blue with dark blue sequined net over silk; beige silk shot with gold and edged with gold embroidery; lavender shot with silver; black shot with copper; fake diamonds competing with real gold jewelry; hair streaked, stretched, pinned, permed and lacquered into place. A roaring gale wouldn't have shifted a single strand.

Elegance personified though, I must admit.

A tall lady, slim, short cropped midnight black hair, huge diamante ear rings, drifts by in a classic black and silver *sari*.

Two Scarlett O'Hara's, one a delicate creature anchored firmly to the ground by an enormous swathe of crimson velvet, the other, a wood nymph in bottle green, they must both be sweltering.

A carrot-haired plump woman who has squeezed herself into a brilliant, orange satin affair is not doing herself any favours, likewise a late teens, maybe early twenties slightly overweight, arrogant, horse faced female, waist length brown hair alternatively streaked henna and blonde, wearing a dress and stole of what can only be described as flashing traffic lights stuck on green, and to top it all, a tiara!

A couple of real Kuchis, dark-skinned, dark-eyed, aquiline faces in Punjabi *joras* of beige and scarlet, pink and blue, stare in horror at a ferocious looking apparition marching through the throng in imitation, traditional Kuchi dress comprised of brightly coloured pieces of velvet, gold braid, mirrors edged with plastic pearls for epaulets, a vivid silk scarf in yellow, orange, pink and purple tied around her head bandana style and scarlet rouge, in perfect rounds on either cheek, giving her the appearance of a toy soldier crossed with a rag doll.

I ask one of the doctor's daughters if the woman is a real Kuchi or not...no...just dress up time.

Come as your own favourite fantasy.

Wide-eyed, and probably open-mouthed, I gaze around the room.

Was I really in Kabul?

Was this really Afghanistan?

Was I awake or lost in some weird dream?

I am the only person in Afghan attire.

Maybe my kind of outfit is relegated to mountain villages by now.

I thought I would blend in.

I don't.

An Annie Lennox try to lookalike who, at fifty something should have known better; creatures with three inch long silver claws; tight, floor length satin skirts in shocking pink, baby-blue edged with fur and slit to the knee revealing net tights on one, a modest white *shalwar* on the other.

Ghararas, Sherwaras, saris, Indian movie actresses crossed with Dallas.

Incredible beehive hairdos, synthetic hairpieces, chestnut ringlets, complicated woven crowns, synthetic white blonde wigs; white shoes

to match white nail polish, white lipstick; everything completely over the top.

Joan Collins, Elizabeth Taylor, Bette Davis, Audrey Hepburn, even Pocahontas in beaded and fringed buckskin was here and this was only the ladies.

Only half of the long room was partially screened off from the men, the dance floor and the very live band being shared by men and women alike.

Of the males, particularly the dancers, there is an eclectic mix of John Travoltas, Zorba the Greeks, Cossacks, Jungle Book *Bhalus* and would-be-*bhangras*.

Every once in a while someone showers them with fistfuls of Afghani notes, children then diving into the fray and returning to the sidelines to compare their hauls with glee. 'I've got 125. I've got 175,' one gap-toothed nine-year-old in drummer boy uniform managed a magnificent 365 and fought to hang on to it when an older boy attempted to extract the crumpled notes from his tightly clenched fist.

DUST MOTES – 16

The bride, in peppermint green lace, her chosen consort in smart suit and broad red tie, known as a 'kipper tie' back in the 1960s, made their triumphal entrance, posed for photographs then retired to a separate room.

'My father made all the arrangements,' one of the doctor's daughters, an English speaker who had automatically attached herself to my side, insisting I join their table, explained.

'The bride is an Afghan American from San Francisco. She is a nurse by profession. Her father passed away years ago and her mother wanted her to marry a proper Afghan man. She wrote to my father and asked him to find some suitable boys. The bride and her mother came to Kabul just last week, chose a boy and now it is their marriage day.'

She didn't find anything unusual about this but I certainly did.

The bride, a statuesque, light brown haired young lady and her equally statuesque mother, wearing a powder blue, well tailored, skirt and jacket, an artistically wrapped white *hijab* and is the spitting image of Angela Lansbury in 'Murder She Wrote', had actually come husband shopping.

'My father arranged a selection of possible husbands and paraded them and their credentials in front of the two women the day after they arrived in Kabul,' the girl continued.

'He did this in a room in his clinic. The two women watched the proceedings from a curtained off section of the room, the place where my father usually examines his patients. The young man of their choice, a former student of my father and now a qualified doctor himself, was happy to be chosen as this means, hopefully, not only has he now got a wife but also a life in America. The bride returns to America next week as she has to go back to work and her new husband will join her as soon as his paper work is done.'

The Pakistani marriage market in reverse!

I have never encountered such a procedure before but my companion told me that it is not an unusual process at all.

How times...and traditions change.

– VI –

The wedding meal was a sumptuous sit down affair rather than the Pakistani style stampede to a buffet to which I have become accustomed.

Twelve people to a table with so many platters of food slammed down by rushing waiters that some were piled on top of each other. Orange *Pilau*, Chicken *Pilau*, Spinach *Pilau*, *Mantu*, *Koftas*, chunks of roast lamb, beef, chicken, salads, *nan*, *kheer*, oranges, bananas, water, Pepsi, green tea.

Dinner was the only sedate event.

Even the band took a break.

Memoona, sitting to one side of me, was looking distinctly worried.

'What is wrong?' I asked.

'It is my mother,' she sheepishly replied going red in the face.

I searched the throng, eventually spotting her roaming from table to table, chatting with this one and that one.

I couldn't see what she was so worried, even embarrassed about.

The band returned with renewed energy, pounding out some pretty good stuff if only the singer would keep his mouth shut.

The drum beat was excellent.

Blood curdling yells, ululations, some recorded, others for real, raised the pace to a frenzy.

The whole building…and my head…throbbed.

The Hordes of Genghis Khan celebrating a victory, an analogy Kabulis wouldn't appreciate as they dislike the Hazaras intensely.

I tried to picture the males present as *Mujahideen*, actually going out and fighting for their country.

Only a meagre one per cent passed my own personal litmus test.

Their gangster style suits and ties, jeans and T-shirts, Doc. Martin boots, just refused to coalesce into the garb of freedom fighters.

I tried supplanting the faces of *Mujahideen* of memory with those dancing before me…it still didn't work.

No Anwars, Gul Ruzs, Telabazs, Karimullahs, Mirwais, even Waliyat Khans here.

I wondered would they alter, transmogrify if necessary.

I hope that neither they, nor I, ever have to find out.

The best dancers were a little boy of six or seven in track suit bottoms and a green nylon T-shirt who could shake it like nothing on earth and an old man who decided to give an impromptu exhibition of traditional dancing which resulted in each man putting one hand on the shoulder of the guy infront, linking up to form a jogging circle, into the centre of which each one had to dance in turn to the cheering, stomping and clapping of the audience.

A quick trip to the outside hallway for some air revealed one of the Titanic girls and her boyfriend in a rather glued together embrace behind a door and a group of twenty something males lacing their cans of Pepsi and Miranda with Russian Vodka.

Back inside, women couldn't resist the beat any longer, here and there one would leap up and dance a frenzy in the women's area of the room then subside in a sweating heap to the enthusiastic, rhythmic table pounding of her friends.

The band switched from modern Afghan to Indian movie music and the Titanic girls burst into action undulating and miming film songs, their actions an indication of the hours and hours spent practicing in front of mirrors at home.

The guys videoing the event, for family consumption only, aimed their cameras in delight.

The bride, now in white lace, and groom reappeared for a circuit of the room, the grinning doctor throwing gold foil wrapped sweets and nuts in all directions at once. The weeping mother holding a lace covered Quran above their heads.

The black and silver *sari* clad woman couldn't contain herself any longer, erupting into a wild dance accompanied, much to my surprise, by an equally gyrating male.

Some of the elderly ladies tut-tutted away, younger ones stared in envy, then two or three other couples joined in.

I wonder how the *Taliban* would have reacted…shot them on the spot I suppose.

I also wondered if all the exuberance had its roots in *Taliban* enforced repression.

'No. It has always been like this,' said my young companion. 'It was like this in my grandmother's time too. We Afghans like to enjoy ourselves.'

An over-blown woman, bulging out of a luminous orange *sari* decided to steal the show and took over the dance floor right in front of the band, the wilder the clapping, the wilder her dance.

A man in a crisp, white, *shalwar kameez* elbowed his way through the crowd.

A new arrival come to take his wife home.

He asked someone where she was and…unluckily for her…was pointed in the dancers direction.

She was lost in a world of her own.

Surrounded by dancing young men showering her with money which children dove for, yet others spraying them all with cans of imitation snow, video crew in overdrive.

The shocked man fought his way through the chaos, grabbed his exhibitionist wife by the hair, hauled her off the dance floor, slapped her hard, strode out and left her to follow.

Everyone froze.

A fight seemed imminent.

She simply shrugged her shoulders, laughed to another guest, disappeared inside a long black coat and left.

I longed to do the same but we were still waiting for our driver to return.

Farhad's girl still hadn't arrived and I didn't think she would.

It was long after midnight and having been advised not to venture out after dark I was worried.

Also, the Kabul TV guy had told me that as unemployment is so high, wages so low, house robberies and hold-ups are common, particularly of wedding guests late at night.

Our driver eventually strolled in, spent almost an hour talking with friends then had to be convinced to leave.

Memoona was looking for her mother again.

I helped and finally spotted her, loaded down with bulging plastic carrier bags, outside the kitchen door.

'Oh no!' said Memoona. 'I knew it!'

Her mother was exceedingly pleased with herself, holding on to her booty with pride.

Food.

It was food.

Pilau, nan, meat, fruit, as much of the wedding cake as she could manage.

'For the children,' she told me, not in the least bit embarrassed.

Food is food after all.

A group of women, including the black and silver *sari* clad dancer, who is a lecturer at Kabul University and had spent a number of years in India, insisted that I go home with them. Spend what was left of the night talking. They would send me back the next day.

I would like to have gone with them.

Exhaustion dictated otherwise.

Plus, there would be panic if I disappeared, and to top it all, I didn't even know the address of 'home'.

Two of the Titanic girls and a brother squeezed into our car, we were to take them to Microrayon.

The doctor and nine other people squashed into his.

Two Toyota Corollas, right-hand drive of course, both with music blasting out into the starlight Kabul night.

The city streets were eerily deserted except for the inevitable.

Convoys of ISAF troops on the prowl.

High-Tech hyenas.

Packs of them hunting in the night.

Far more than during the daytime.

Automatic rifle fire from somewhere close by.

A rocket explosion in the distance.

It was frightening.

I needed the security of my own den.

Our crazy driver decided to race the doctor, he responded with fervour.

I hit the roof, quite literally, more than once, where unseen speed breakers lay in wait.

I was petrified of an accident.

I had been in one some months previously in Pakistan.

A whump, a thud, the implosion of shattered glass and my world changed in seconds.

I didn't want this to happen again.

I lost my temper.

Threatened the idiot with dire consequences if he didn't slow down.

If Anwar didn't shoot him then I would.

He slowed down then raced again and it wasn't until I demanded he stop and find me a taxi that he listened.

If I had arrived back in a taxi then all hell would have been let loose.

The grinning doctor insisted we have tea in his apartment but I adamantly refused, much to the disappointment of Memoona and her mother.

Instead, I was taken to their house as their brother was now frightened of bumping into Anwar if he delivered me back himself.

'You must stay the night,' mumbled Farhad's girl from where she had been dozing on a mattress in the minute, lace and crochet shrouded living room.

The trappings of Central European homes all around.

Nothing Asian in sight.

'No. I must get back.' I insisted as I needed sleep, a good sleep and certainly wouldn't manage it under these conditions no matter how welcoming my intended hosts.

'I will phone for Farhad,' she said.

He arrived, along with Sabir, cursing the party, the work, the lateness of the hour and I couldn't blame him.

His girl hastily packed a small bag and joined us.

Thankfully it wasn't far.

I eventually arrived back around 3 a.m., completely exhausted, stressed out and with a blinding headache to boot.

'Sabir and I just finished cleaning your room,' Farhad told me trying to focus his bloodshot eyes. 'There were bottles, rice, glasses, cans, ashtrays all over the place.'

The garden was a bomb site.

About thirty ministers along with various directors of various departments and their bodyguards had had a riotous time...complete with musicians, singing...Black Label, Russian Vodka, beer and wine.

Apparently their regular Thursday night party moves from host to host and house to house.

This had been Anwar's turn.

The Afghan hierarchy in action and I missed it!

END OF PART FIVE

PART SIX

– I –

Dust haze.

Fragmented sunshine illuminates a whole gang of Hazaras, including women in blouses, mid-calf length black skirts, white *shalwars* and matching headscarves, engrossed in a major clean up operation out on the lawn.

It resembles a scene from southern Turkey.

Workers on a farm I visited in Anatolia.

There they were washing newly harvested olives then crushing them by hand with wooden mallets.

Here they are tackling a mountain of pots and pans under the hosepipe in the centre of the wrecked lawn.

There is water everywhere.

Their clothing is soaked.

They are having a wonderful time.

Laughter fills the exhausted atmosphere.

Joking men, rolled-up trousers and jeans, rolled-up shirt sleeves, short-sleeved T-shirts, barefoot, are cleaning carpets, chairs, tables, sweeping up rice, broken glasses, beer cans, dumping the debris into a tin hip bath, used for ice the previous night and currently already full to overflowing with empty bottles of booze.

The bathroom is being disinfected and the kitchen hosed down.

There is no sign of Farhad and his girl.

No sound from their room.

I imagine that there are a lot of people sleeping it off this morning.

The aftermath of Thursday night in Kabul.

I am sitting on my mattress sipping coffee…thinking.

One of the Hazaras knocks politely on my open door.

'Yes,' I answer.

He steps warily into the room, telling me that he would like to talk.

Squatting on his haunches just inside the doorway and looking at the floor, the walls, the ceiling, out of the windows, looking anywhere except directly at me as is correct, he tells me his story.

DUST MOTES – 17

Born near Shibarghan area of Jowzjan province in the north of the country, Karim, a Shia somewhere in his late thirties, is a smallish, delicate boned man with the high cheekbones and tilted dark eyes of his race.

'I was a small boy, less than ten years old when the *Peshmerga* came,' he recollected.

His use of the word '*Peshmerga*' intrigued me.

It is a Kurdish term meaning 'Those who are ready to die'.

I can only presume that he was referring to *Mujahideen*.

None of the *Mujahideen* factions, large or small, splinter groups or otherwise, were angels but this was the first time I have personally heard an individual's account of the terrible atrocities laid directly at their feet.

'They killed so many people in my village. Raped my mother and elder sister in front of my father…Then cut open their stomachs… Then cut their throats. It is because we are Hazara and we are also Shia,' he adds shaking his head in remembered despair and continuing anguish.

'Then I went with my two older brothers and younger sisters to my grandfather's home and we stayed there and helped him with his land and his sheep.

It was difficult.

Sometimes the *Peshmerga* came and sometimes they didn't.

When we saw them we ran away and hid in a small hole that my grandfather made.

We all hid.

A branch with some grass was pulled over the hole.

Sometimes we stayed there for three or four days.

We had a jar of water, some dried nuts and fruit.

They destroyed my grandfather's farm many times but we still lived and made a new home out of trees, mud and grass.'

I wondered how he could sit in a house belonging to a former *Mujahideen* commander and speak of such things without obvious fear.

Anwar's group did not operate in the Shibarghan area.

To the best of my knowledge, that area was often controlled by the notorious General Dostum...but not always...it changed hands on numerous occasions.

I do not know, for certain, exactly who he was speaking of.

Perhaps Naeem had told him that I am a Shia too.

Perhaps this is why he wanted to tell me his story.

'Then, sometime later, some years later, the *Taliban* came,' he continued his shocking account.

'They killed my grandfather so my grandmother brought us to Kabul where we lived in a mud hut on a mountain near the city.

'We tried to find work but nobody like Hazara people because we are Shia and have "*Chine*" eyes.'

Karim squints out to where his companions are spraying each other with the hosepipe.

The ghost of a smile briefly flickers across his almost impassive features.

'One day I am at the *adda* and some *Taliban* come.

They see me and make me come to them.

I have cigarette packet in my chemise pocket and they see this.

This is *Taliban* time and cigarette is forbidden.

They slap me hard like this'. Tuc...Tuc, he demonstrates.

'On the face.

Then they make me eat five cigarettes until packet is empty.

Then eat packet too.

Next they make all people to stand one hundred feet away in circle and they make me dance with pistol.

Then they see I am good dancer...no bullet in my feet.

They hit me to the mud and go away.

No cigarette...ever again!

In night-time I leave and walk over mountains to Pakistan.

Now I came, twenty days ago, to visit my relatives.

I work in bed sheet factory in Karachi.

My wife and children are in Karachi.

It took three days by bus.

Rs 500 from Karachi to Peshawar. Rs 50 from Peshawar to Torkham. Rs 150 from Torkham to Kabul.

After one week I go back to Karachi.

American Army is in Kabul so okay for now but still no one like Hazara Shia people.

In five years again there will be '*Jang*' and again Hazara people will have bad time.

I stay with my family in Karachi.

Is this better or I try to go to Iran...that is more better for Shia people?'

I advise him that Afghan refugees in Iran are being sent back to Afghanistan…so are refugees from Pakistan.

Both countries have extended their hospitality and aid to millions of Afghans for years now and their respective governments consider it safe for them to go home, return to Afghanistan now that reconstruction is underway.

'But this is not true for Hazara Shias,' he says in disappointment.

I remind him that in 2002, for the first time in over twenty years, Shias were allowed to express their mourning for the members of the Prophet's (PBUH) family massacred near Karbala in present day Iraq 1,3000 years ago in AH 61/680 CE, during Muharram and to practice ritual flagellation on Ashura in Kabul.

In a show of solidarity, religious freedom, even President Karzai, a Sunni, attended Chendaul Mosque, along with thousands of Shia men and women on that historic day.

'This was good,' he solemnly agrees. 'It is our right but when the fighting starts again, as it will, then again we will be victimized. It is not good to be Hazara or Shia in Afghanistan.'

I do not know what else to say.

He sits in silence for a few minutes, brow furrowed in concentration, eyes seeing a different horizon than the one offered by this room.

'I will have to think about this,' he says rising slowly to his feet, pulling at his extremely sparse beard.

'I will talk with my relatives then I will go back to Karachi and think.'

– II –

Farhad and his girl finally emerge.

Both yawning, both red-eyed, both unsmiling.

Maybe they've had an argument.

Maybe that back room is sound proof as I didn't hear a thing.

She takes over the bathroom.

Hauling out the washing machine and filling the bath tub with water.

She is doing Farhad's weekly wash and looks about ready to fall into the machine with it.

Her eyes are hanging on her cheekbones.

The machine whirrs, slaps, buzzes.

She hauls out the wet clothes, wrings them with tired hands, tosses them into the bath-tub to rinse.

Wrings them out again, dumps them in a bucket, goes out and flings them over the washing line at the side of the lawn.

No pegs.

They are sure to blow off.

Sweating profusely, T-shirt and jeans stuck tight to her 'spare tyres' she asks if I need anything ironed.

I do.

I prefer to do it myself though.

She crawls into the sparkling clean kitchen.

Emerges with heaped plates of warmed up Kabuli *Pilau*.

Last night's leftovers.

Mouth-wateringly delicious.

Farhad is expecting visitors.

Four Afghan Canadians.

He spirits his girl away before they arrive.

She seems relieved to go.

I'm absolutely fed up.

I would go and visit Gul Ruz but don't know the way.

I ask Waliyat Khan.

'You can't go out alone,' he tells me in a tone of voice which doesn't allow for dispute.

'Gul Ruz's *buccha* will come and pick you up later. I forgot to tell you before.'

The afternoon stretches.

I doze a while.

Time shrinks.

Decide to freshen up my 'Meet the President outfit' just in case its needed.

Iron the black *shalwar*, dusty pink silk chemise, matching embroidered waistcoat.

Take out my precious, pink shaded, crocheted silk Victorian shawl.

Find that the moths have been at it.

Must fumigate my wardrobe when I go home.

Take out my emergency sewing kit, darn one hole after another.

Pass another hour in the process.

House arrest is boring!

The Parwan Wind gathers strength again.

Whistles through the *jali* across the windows.

Rattles the doors.

Dust devils pirouette in the driveway.

The carpet in here was vacuumed this morning but I already leave footprints on its dust impregnated surface as I pace the room in a vain attempt at restoring circulation to my cramped limbs.

I am not used to this inactivity.

Farhad insists that the dust is because of so many destroyed buildings combined with their reconstruction.

These may well be contributing factors but I do recall, belatedly, that I read somewhere or other, that Kabul has always been like this.

Dry.

Dusty.

Crazy.

This brings me to another point.

The destruction of West Kabul by warring factions of *Mujahideen* is a blatant reality.

Most, if not all, other areas of the city display bullet-marked, rocket-damaged and shrapnel-pocked buildings but why do the media only concentrate on these?

Why do they largely ignore the buildings, of all kinds which are springing up?

Marble-faced monstrosities with reflecting glass windows.

Tasteful bungalows with newly planted trees.

Large and small apartment blocks and none of these in small numbers.

The city is being rebuilt and redesigned at the same time.

Mud houses and *havelis* being replaced by modern constructions.

Whether the inhabitants are the same or not I don't know but imagine that land grabbers have had, are having a field day ever since the Saur Revolution back in 1978 when the first exodus began.

Returning refugees may well find a palatial palace replacing the modest '*kuccha*' homes they left behind, and I expect, there won't be a damn thing they can do about it either.

All over the city there is a roaring trade in building material; cement, wood, door and window frames, bricks, sand, stone, gravel.

Lower down the financial scale there are mountains of broken bricks, splintered timbers with stories to tell, anything reusable, recyclable for those on a budget.

Mud, dung, long straw and short straw for those on the bottom rung.

Empty shipping containers are used as homes, stores, some mud plastered and thatched to keep out the heat of summer, the cold of winter.

I hear stories, echoes of stories of there previous use.

'Prisoners were kept in them by different groups of *Mujahideen*,' says Waliyat Khan.

'Some mad people, sick in the head people, fired Kalashnikovs into the trapped prisoners. Just shot them down. Murdered them. Some even fired rocket-propelled grenades inside. After this there is nothing left. Not even pieces. Not a single finger, not an ear. Those were terrible times. I was not here. I was still in Haripur in Pakistan. I can not even think about such things now.'

I know that hundred upon hundred Hazara Shias died in shipping containers.

Herded in like cattle by the *Taliban* in Mazar-i-Sharif.

Men, women and children.

The containers dispatched to distant destinations.

The prisoners without food or water dying terrible deaths on the way.

Atrocities which no one likes to think about.

Atrocities which really happened here.

Atrocities happen somewhere on the planet every single second of every single day and none of us likes to imagine how it would feel if we personally, family, friends, acquaintances, had to undergo them ourselves.

The reality is horrendous.

– III –

The impression that Farhad has been sent to Kabul to kick his heels increases daily.

His position here is ambiguous.

He is Anwar's nephew so, outwardly, people respect him.

He looks after this house, has a huge television with lots of satellite channels, an impressive music system, a mobile phone which is always in use, use of a car, beer and Black Label in his room yet no visible form of income.

He swears like a trooper when he thinks no one is around.

I heard him through the *jali* window this afternoon when he thought I was sleeping.

Seeing off his Afghan Canadian friends.

'I don't have any time f...time for those shit-eating mother f...from New York who come here speaking f...shit...know what I f... mean?'

Embarrassed laughs from his 'friends' who left without wishing him 'goodbye'.

Farhad putting on the big man style, discovering the coat doesn't fit, suffering a private agony which doesn't allow him to smoke in front of Anwar.

He doesn't understand why I am shown respect by people such as Commander Telabaz when they have none for his fiancé.

Nor does he comprehend why Anwar, even though he doesn't have time himself, is making sure that I am taken care of.

Transport, guards, drivers with strict instructions to go where I want unless it is too dangerous, armed with guns, money to buy drinks, food for them and me, money for fuel if needed.

Just yesterday Farhad asked me how long I had been in Jegdalek with the *Mujahideen*.

He has recently read *The Gun Tree* but still can't figure out a time-frame, and over the years he has heard me spoken of, knew that I had been in London with Arif and another sister, Reega, that I'd flown there from Muscat when Reega went for medical treatment, that I'd visited them in Peshawar, that Anwar had visited me in Scotland.

He is confused.

He can't pin me down.

Apparently I am to be given VIP treatment at the airport when I leave on Monday.

I don't understand it all myself!

Gul Ruz's son, Khair Muhammad, didn't arrive.

The mystery man from Mazar-i-Sharif did.

DUST MOTES – 18

Slim built, of medium height, dressed in black from head to toe the stranger, a mobile phone glued to his ear, was leaning against the open front door when I emerged from the kitchen, tray of green tea in my hands.

'Is that for me?' he asked, raising his eyebrows quizzically. 'How thoughtful.'

I handed over my refreshment, returned to the kitchen and made some more.

Mr Ahmad Shah Obeid, an Afghan born, London based political analyst, here to have a second round of meetings with President Karzai and the sidelined Professor Rabbani.

'Had meetings with them both early last week. Before I headed up to Mazar-i-Sharif to take a look around,' he told me still brushing the dust of his day-long return journey off his clothes.

'Lunatic drivers here,' he said in disgust.

'They don't even know which side of the road to drive on so they drive in the middle. You can't guess which side they will swerve towards when they meet a vehicle coming from the opposite direction. The roads are absolute death traps.'

He speaks precise, top drawer English, with a rather bland accent and reminds me of the character in an old television advertisement for a particular brand of dark chocolate.

'The man with the black magic box' who delivered his gift by parachute, dangling from a helicopter, abseiling down sheer cliffs.

But...this man is extremely bitter.

Disillusioned.

'Karzai wants me to join his government but he is so naive, so stupid, that I am not even sure if I want to meet with him again,' he informs me, grimacing in disgust, lounging against cushions in my room, sipping my tea.

Invading my space.

Breaking the monotony.

Mr Obeid left Kabul over twenty years ago.

'My father decided it was time to get out. Leave while we still could,' he justified. 'He felt that we might lose everything if we stayed. Those were dark days for everyone.'

Dark days indeed.

Particularly for those who chose to stay...and for those who elected to fight.

Even darker for those without an option.

'You could have stayed,' I told him, wanting to gauge his reaction.

He raises his eyebrows, sips tea, considers how to reply.

'I was only 18 or 19,' he eventually says. 'I had to do as my father told me.'

I very much doubted that.

Many *Mujahideen* were much, much younger.

'Anyway,' he continued. 'It was more important for me to complete my education, prepare myself to help Afghanistan when I could. Our country needs educated people now...so...after twenty years of waiting...I am here.'

He smiles broadly.

Expecting to be congratulated.

About 40 years of age, handsome in a rugged kind of way.

Oozing self-confidence from the deep creases in his forehead.

He lives between London, Brighton and Devon, has a home in Spain, an apartment in Dubai.

He is in the upmarket sports car trade.

'I have a good life,' he reflects. 'My wife and son want for nothing.'

'I really want to do something for my country now but the level of corruption here is horrific. There is also a total lack of political acumen.'

He shakes his head, runs fingers through his hair, exhales angrily.

'All we have right now is corrupt bastards who just want to fill their pockets and run, and as for Karzai...he would do better running Kentucky Fried Chicken than trying to run Afghanistan. Hell. If the man can't even organize his own security with his own people but has to depend on Americans then what kind of weak person is he?'

I shrug my shoulders.

I am not expected to answer.

'Afghanistan would respond to a strong leader. Basically the people here will respect someone they can look up to but that respect must be earned and this takes time. Afghan people respond to a personality not to politics but they also need to see that that person is really achieving things for the country.

I have spoken with people from all walks of life, crippled beggars in Mazar-i-Sharif, shopkeepers, truckers, etc., etc. and have discovered that absolutely everyone is totally confused about what is going on.'

He cites a much publicized opium poppy eradication programme.

'Things like that UN poppy programme were a crazy mistake. The idiots actually paying farmers $10,000 a hectare not to grow poppy or to destroy their existing poppy crop. Obviously this encouraged those who were growing grain and vegetables to switch to opium poppies in order to get $10,000 in their hands. Far, far more than they could dream of getting for growing food crops and far less work. This stupid, ill-thought of course of action only served to drastically increase poppy production not reduce it!'

I wonder at the lunacy of it myself.

He switches track, talking in overdrive, an exhausted reaction to everything he has heard, witnessed during his visit and trip up country.

'Take Karzai,' he shakes his head, slops tea over the rim of his cup, coughs.

'Damn dust,' he curses before continuing with his tirade.

'Yes. Karzai. He is currently renegotiating with exactly the same bastards he formerly got rid of as there isn't anyone else. He is also renegotiating with foreign governments. With individuals who open talks by saying "How much will you pay me first, cash in hand, in advance and then we will tell you what to do?" Everyone takes the money and runs. Very few actually deliver anything feasible at all. It is all money, power and greed.'

I wonder where Anwar fits in.

He's in something up to his neck, that's for sure.

Busy politicking from morning to night and back again.

His family is safely stashed in London.

He could walkout anytime.

On deeper reflection...he's not the type to run.

He hasn't done so before.

I think.

– IV –

Farhad finally returned.

Kindly brought me an Afghan burger.

Hard-boiled eggs, French fries, smoked sausage, salami, tomato sauce, all precariously wrapped in a *roti*.

Mr Obeid stared at the concoction dubiously.

'I wouldn't eat that if I were you,' he advised. 'You'll be sick for a month. Stick to plain *kebabs*. Much safer.'

Farhad was hurt.

It showed.

'What on earth are you doing here alone anyway?' Mr Obeid demanded as he finished his tea, stone cold by now as was my own. 'Afghanistan is far too dangerous for a woman, especially on her own. Your husband shouldn't have allowed you to come.'

'Banafsha was with the *Mujahideen* during the Russian time,' Farhad throws in. 'That was more dangerous than now.'

'I wouldn't be so sure of that,' Mr Obeid dryly observes rising to his feet. 'Kabul must be one of the most dangerous places on earth.'

'I came to do some research,' I defend myself. 'To interview Anwar and others from the Jegdalek days.'

'Why do you want to waste your time interviewing him?' he retorts. 'He's a nobody. Not important.'

I don't enlarge.

I've had enough for one day.

He disappears off to the television room, commandeering a bottle of my precious herbal cough syrup on the way.

Arrogant and proud of it.

Afghan to the core.

I don't think he would have lasted long in Jegdalek

Far too basic for him.

I was hungry.

I ate the burger and lived!

END OF PART SIX

PART SEVEN

– I –

The tension is palpable this morning.

Even 'The Parwan Wind' is holding its breath.

I am not the only one waiting for Anwar to arrive.

Farhad is in and out as usual.

Waliyat Khan is pacing up and down outside the entrance gate.

Naeem is watering what remains of the lawn and hosing down the walls and driveway.

Mr Obeid, television blaring, has been joined by a tatty looking scarecrow in regulation 1950s style suit, a portly, grey haired guy in a decent suit, white shirt and daffodil yellow tie and a couple of other characters whom I can hear but not see.

They don't appear to have entered through the door, maybe they confirmed Waliyat Shah's fears and climbed over the back wall.

They certainly didn't come down the non-existent chimney!

They are sitting, cross-legged around a flower-patterned plastic tablecloth spread out on the floor, stuffing their faces with mangoes and fresh *nan*, drinking Pepsi. Arguing about something or other in Dari.

Waliyat Khan tried to get me to eat two mangoes and a *nan*.

'Mangoes make you strong the doctor told me,' he announced indicating my car accident weakened arm. 'Very good medicine for you.'

Two huge mangoes...I'd probably end up spending the day in the bathroom and don't want to risk that.

One mango and half a *nan* dipped in coffee is more than enough for me.

I take my finished breakfast tray into the kitchen, and as I step barefoot back towards my room a voice interrupts my train of thought.

'You are wearing Afghan clothes. Very nice indeed.'

It is Mr Yellow Tie calling from the facing room.

'Pakistani,' I haughtily correct him, turning to enter my door.

'Definitely Afghan,' he insists as I close him out.

Farhad knocks timidly on my closed door.

'Banafsha?' he queries. 'It's okay Banafsha. He didn't mean to be rude. He was just complimenting you that's all.'

The endless waiting is obviously taking its toll on my nerves.

'When will Anwar arrive?' I ask.

'Soon Banafsha. Very soon,' Farhad insists. 'These guys are waiting for him too. They have all come from London for a meeting.'

I promptly envisage my promised two-hour interview evaporating.

Anwar has far more important things to do than be interviewed by me.

'When will he come?'

'He said by 11 a.m.,' Farhad answers.

'Keep calm Banafsha. Just keep calm. He is coming. I promise.'

I've heard it all before.

Too many times before.

Half-an-hour later Farhad and the two invisible men disappear.

The television is switched off.

The voices of Mr Obeid and Mr Yellow tie rumble on.

Waliyat Khan polishes his Kalashnikov.

Naeem waters the grass...again.

He should be watering vegetables, flowers, fruit, herbs not grass and concrete.

What a waste.

Loudspeakers on the road in the world outside the gate.

A VIP coming from or going to the airport.

I finally learnt why I must lock everything in my suitcase...even when going to the loo.

The pock-faced young man acting as Mr Obeid's driver appropriated his camera, rummaged through all of his belongings when he stayed here last week.

I would have fired the guy but apparently there are 'political implications'.

He is the son of some important person and the relative of others.

A spoilt brat and a thief.

11.30 a.m. Still no sign of Anwar.

Farhad returns.

Mr Obeid introduces Mr Yellow tie.

'This is Mr Aman, Banafsha. The former President of Afghan Ariana Airways. He has been requested to consider taking his old position back so has come for a look around first.'

They return to the television room.

I return to my mattress from where I can see the front gate.

More strangers arrive.

I turn over my conversation with Mr Obeid last night.

He claimed that the assassination of Ahmad Shah Massoud on 9 September 2001 was a joint Al-Qaeda, ISI operation.

If this is true, then no wonder so many Afghans hate Pakistan despite the millions who were given refuge there.

Yes.

We all know that the *Taliban* were created and funded by Pakistan and Saudi Arabia back when Benazir Bhutto ruled the roost but...I find it difficult to accept that the assassination of charismatic Massoud was to pave the way for a Caliphate, a pure Islamic State, a new home for the Islamic faith here in Afghanistan.

I know that Pakistan, Saudi Arabia and the United Arab Emirates were the only ones to acknowledge *Taliban* rule here and that Professor Rabbani retained his United Nations seat throughout but, if Al-Qaeda and the ISI did have a hand in the assassination then they helped pave the way for American intervention and the end of a Caliphate.

Besides this...did Pakistan really want a pure *Taliban* state on its northern doorstep?

Maybe we did.

I'm not a politician or a military strategist.

Perhaps both Pakistan and Saudi Arabia underestimated the monster they unleashed.

However, it is America which excels in this...be it in Iraq, South America or wherever.

America, as I understand it, had already made plans to 'intervene' in Afghanistan well before the terrible happenings of 11 September 2001 which served as a timely excuse.

They needed a base here.

Not just for the exploitation of minerals etc.

They need a centre from which to extend their tentacles into the Central Asian States, Iran, Pakistan and get further to grips with India.

They most certainly do not want Afghanistan, Iran, Pakistan, Turkey, Tajikistan, Uzbekistan, Kyrgyzstan to form an Islamic Alliance. Iran, Pakistan and Turkey having tried, and failed, to do this in the past, well before anyone of them had gone nuclear.

I don't suppose that China wants this either.

They already have enough on their plate trying to keep a lid on Muslim majority provinces such as Xingjian, the home province of my husband's paternal grandmother.

I wonder if our family are still banned from there by the way?

'The Great Game' continues...only the players are new...particularly the American card be it The Joker, The Fool, The Hanged Man, The Tower of Destruction, Death wielding his reapers scythe or all of these put together.

I'm getting in over my head now.

It's all this damned waiting!

– II –

Mr Obeid and Mr Aman leave...return.

Farhad goes back out.

'Anwar Shah is coming,' says Mr Obeid sticking his head around my door. 'Soon'.

12 noon and counting.

Wonder if the garden isn't planted due to lack of interest, lack of time, prospect of another war or the prospect of Anwar, pockets full, doing a runner.

Or, is Anwar politicking for a higher position?

More power, more influence, more money?

Let's face it...what do I really know of the man?

Actually...very little indeed.

In 1983 he was Mohammad Anwar, Jamiat-i-Islami *Mujahideen* Commander of Jegdalek Front.

He did not appear, in anyway, to be a rich man.

Urbane...middle class...not from a wealthy background at all.

He had obviously come up in the world when we met in Peshawar early in 1992, if the two-house compound the family then lived in was a source of financial measure.

Okay. At the end of the airport runway not in Hayatabad or some other upmarket area of the city but still, from what I know of Peshawar accommodation prices, not a low cost property at all.

In April 1992, when the *Mujahideen* captured Kabul and Professor Rabbani eventually became Interim President the following year, Anwar, still simply Mohammad Anwar then, was offered the position of Minister for Martyrs and Orphans, a position he refused telling me, in Scotland in 1994, that his reason for refusal was that he didn't 'agree with the situation'.

After the fall of the *Taliban*, historic 13 November 2001, he was appointed to the extremely lucrative, powerful position of 'Mayor of Kabul', and as far as I can work out, this is when he suddenly opted to be known as Mohammad Anwar Jekdalek although, quite possibly, the 'Jekdalek' was a necessary addition in moving his family to London where everyone is expected to have a second name.

Also appointed President of the Olympic Committee of Afghanistan and Director of Physical Education during the same period. Always something of a sportsman, this I can relate to.

According to Mr 'Dashti', Anwar relinquished his position as Mayor in April 2004 when he was appointed as a 'Special Advisor' to Karzai instead.

However, in August 2003 I clearly recall reading of a land grabbing scandal, said to involve the Mayor along with a number of other powerful dignitaries, which was under investigation.

Now I suddenly hear the term 'Anwar Shah' in use and can't help but ponder if it is purely honorific or if there is even more to the already confusing, yet insubstantial, picture.

1.20 p.m. and all hell is suddenly let loose.

A jade green Pajero swarming with guards, yet more uniformed, gun-totting men spilling out of additional vehicles, fills the driveway.

Pandemonium erupts.

Bowing and scraping all round.

I sit on my mattress and watch the spectacle unfold.

Anwar has arrived...en masse.

They treat him like royalty.

How much time will he spare for me?

Certainly not the promised two hours, more like two minutes...let's see.

He and his crowd of courtiers disappear into the television room where I can hear lunch already being taken in.

This is really infuriating and such a bloody waste of time.

An eternity passed as I sat immobile...waiting.

Waiting and wondering.

In reality it was only ten minutes before Anwar, accompanied by Mr Airline, entered my room.

Mr Airline would interpret for us Anwar explained.

I was surprised.

We didn't need an interpreter at all.

Then realized...the presence of a third person was for 'correctness' as, even with the door open, our meeting may have been misconstrued.

My notebook, pens, tape recorder, extra tapes had been ready and waiting for days.

Anwar settled himself at the other end of my mattress.

Mr Airline cross-legged on the floor facing us.

An inquisitorial triangle.

I am unaccountably and very suddenly nervous.

Anwar

'Tell me about yourself Anwar,' I ask as he stares at my small tape recorder as if it is going to jump up and bite him.

He faces tape recorders, interviews, journalists everyday.

He has no reason to be afraid of mine.

'I was born in Kabul in February 1954,' he discloses, starting at the beginning as I have requested.

This short sentence startles me.

I had always been under the impression that he came from Jegdalek.

'What is your connection with Jegdalek?' I enquire as he stares down through the years of memory, seeing pictures that he is reluctant to share.

'Jegdalek was my father's place,' he eventually says.

'What happened to the house there? The one I saw in its orchard of pomegranate trees with the unexploded bomb?'

I immediately envisage Jonsey, Commander Telabaz now, standing the unexploded ordinance on its nose for a photograph. Lunacy!

'This is all destroyed. There is nothing there. I have sent some trees for planting so that there is some greenery but there are too many mines.'

He echoes Gul Ruz on this subject.

'From birth up to the revolution we lived in Kabul. Jegdalek was just a sometimes place.'

'What do you remember of your childhood Anwar? Any particular incident? Anything important?'

He chews thoughtfully on his full-bottom lip considering my question.

'I am trying to think,' he says after a prompt from Mr Airline who is vastly enjoying his unnecessary role. 'There are different types of things that I have in my mind. I went to school, had a lot of friends so did a lot of socializing and also enjoyed sports in school, college and university. So, sometimes sports, sometimes walking here and there, a little bit of kite flying, lots of football, volleyball.'

He paints an ordinary boyhood, a completely ordinary life.

He is not an ordinary man.

'In Kabul University I studied philosophy, literature, Persian, Pashto and Arabic which I have forgotten,' he adds hastily. 'So much I have forgotten. It is only now that I can find a little time for literature again. I get classical books, like *The Three Musketeers* in Persian from Iran.'

'How did you become involved in politics?' I query, switching track towards the things I really want to know.

'By force,' he answers simply. 'By force when the Russians came and took over Afghanistan.'

'But the *Mujahideen* movement started before that,' I counter. 'The revolution happened before the Russians came.'

'That is true Banafsha but I was not involved previously. I was in the Student Union at University, I was pushed into this by friends. They were against the communist parties and so was I.'

'He was also a member of the Olympic group in the university,' interjects Mr Airline. 'The National Committee.'

I ignore him.

'How did you come to leave Kabul and go to fight in Jegdalek? How did that happen?'

Mr Airline takes over again.

'In 1980 when Russians took over the country, at that time there was Olympic Games in Moscow. He was appointed in Olympic Committee but I think that they cancelled his name and tell him that he can't say that he comes from Afghanistan. He start the *Jihad* from that time.'

Mr Airline beams proudly in Anwar's direction, silently seeking approval for deflecting my questions.

Anwar gives me a quick, under the lashes, glance of apology...or is it amusement?

'Actually I had a connection with Ahmad Shah Massoud,' he tells me directly. 'At that time he was in Panjshir valley so I got on a bus and travelled there to discuss the situation with him. When I returned to Kabul I came to know that KHAD and Russian service were following me, watching me all the time. I gave this matter some more thought and decided to go first to Paktia, then to Zazi and onwards, on foot, to Pakistan.'

I remember that route well.

It is the same route that I had travelled, on foot and on horseback, from Pakistan to Jegdalek and back again.

Mr Airline is hungry for details of the journey.

We do not need them.

'What did you discuss with Ahmad Shah Massoud?' I continue, probing gently, a dentist extracting a stubborn tooth.

Anwar has never liked talking.

Especially about himself.

He is a difficult interview.

'I discussed many things including that I was on the Olympic Committee and that they, the Russians, want to send me outside Afghanistan for sports and that I didn't want to go to Moscow at this time. I asked him what I should do and Massoud advised me to go to Pakistan. He gave me a letter of introduction to Professor Rabbani in Peshawar. So I went to Pakistan, saw Professor Rabbani and started *Jihad* from there.

Before leaving, I first took all of my family to safety in Jegdalek. It was much better for them to be outside Kabul when the Russians discovered that I had left, then they could have made a big problem for my family members. When I came back from Pakistan then I shifted all of my family from Jegdalek to Peshawar. This was in the middle of 1980.'

'When I went to Peshawar in 1983 you were all living in tents in the courtyard of a large house,' I remind him. 'How many years did you stay there?'

He chews his lip again, stares at a persistent fly buzzing against the *jali*, mutters to Mr Airline who replies for him.

'He has forgotten this but for a long time they were in the tents,' he tells me whilst fiddling with his dazzling tie. 'At that time there was nothing for *Mujahideen* so there was not any possibility that they could move. After that...after a long time...they moved from there.'

'Next time I saw you Anwar, in 1992, you were in that house behind Star Petrol Station in Peshawar and you were leaving the next morning for Afghanistan.'

He nods agreement wondering what I am getting at.

'I need to know lots of small things Anwar,' I explain, hoping that I can get him to talk more freely.

He is being awkward.

He confers with Mr Airline in hushed whispers, speaking Dari which he knows, or thinks he knows, I don't understand.

'It would be much better if I spend sometime and write down everything that Mr Jekdalek wants to say,' Mr Airline insistently tells me. 'You just give me a list of questions and I will do this when I have time.'

No way!

I need to talk to Anwar directly not through an intermediary who will write what he wants...if anything at all.

They confer again.

The clatter of plates, cutlery reminds them that lunch is waiting.

'Just a few minutes more,' I insist. 'You promised two hours Anwar not two minutes.'

He looks uncomfortable.

They confer again.

Mr Airline continues without being asked. 'From the beginning he say he was involved in politics by force because he don't want to come to politics but this war came by force. We don't want to make a war and make a fight with our brothers. The other things...when revolution is finished and when *Mujahideen* took over Kabul, I put down all the guns and everything. I stopped from there because I don't want to be involved in that in-fighting from beginning. All my *Mujahideen* were then everywhere and I told them that I will put the guns to the government. I will give all the guns to the government and stop this fighting now.'

This is one of the periods of time that I need detailed information on.

Four terrible, blood thirsty years of civil war.

Everyone wanting control.

Thousands of innocent people killed in Kabul alone.

Unbelievable atrocities.

Unutterable crimes against humanity.

Mujahideen turned into animals.

Tearing each others throats out along with those of anyone else who happened to get in the way.

Rape, pillage, torture.

I was personally so disgusted, wrenched to the soul by the newspaper reports that I read that I stopped.

Just like that.

Tried to put Afghanistan out of my head.

Tried, like the rest of the world to forget that it ever existed.

That I had ever gone there.

That I had so vehemently and vociferously supported the *Mujahideen* in the face of public, family opposition.

Thanked God that I hadn't gone with Anwar from Peshawar back to Afghanistan on the eve of their 'victory'.

For the sake of my own selfish salvation...I needed to know.

Anwar tells me nothing.

Shakes his head.

Looks at me blankly.

Clicks his prayer beads.

Helps himself to one of my cigarettes.

To my lighter.

He is poised for flight.

'When did you move to London?' I ask him, trying to prevent his departure.

His face is tortured.

His thoughts are chasing one another on a gristly merry-go-round.

This is how it appears to me but it could be my own imagination.

'In *Taliban* time,' he finally croaks. 'When *Taliban* take over Afghanistan.'

'He went to London and settle there and after he start the politics again,' Mr Airline jumps to the rescue. 'He is a member of the Bonn Conference. Also in Rome for Zahir Shah group. He was also a member of that group for the democracy. He was also a member of the meeting in Istanbul. He joined these meetings for the democracy of Afghanistan. Different politicians like Mr Karzai, Abdul Haq, Abdullah...these people were with him and he worked for democracy,' the 'praise singer' rolls on.

'Are you related to Zahir Shah, Anwar?'

'No. He don't have any family relationship with Zahir Shah but only he is the former King of Afghanistan. He is an old man...like *Baba*.'

I try again.

'When the *Mujahideen* came to Kabul did your family return?'

'No. They stayed in Pakistan at first.' He is wary of me.

He no longer lounges on the mattress.

His back is straight, legs braced at the knee, ready to rise.

To walk away.

Mr Airline fills the gap.

'When *Mujahideen* come to Kabul he came alone but then the family also came to Kabul,' he explains. 'But when Hekmatyar came here and sit on the mountain and fly those bloody rockets they go back!' He demonstrates, pretends to be flying a rocket, dives pointed hands through the dense atmosphere, makes a sound of explosion, breaks the tension.

I retreat...for the time being.

'Where did you live in London?'

'Greenford,' Anwar says, speaking to me in person again. 'Then Southhall. There are some houses for refugees there. My wife and four children live in one house, my sisters and mother live in another.'

'What of the situation in Afghanistan now Anwar? What do you feel about the American troops and ISAF being here? Do you approve of this or not?'

Resorting to eager Mr Airline again, he replies, 'He says that when *Jihad* is over and we took over Kabul and other provinces in Afghanistan, at that time, between all parties, there was a lot of fighting and they can't do something for the people, at all sides some fighting. Then, after that the *Taliban* came and helped these Al-Qaeda and other groups. Now with these international forces here, this is the need...to help Afghanistan.' He backtracks, leaps forwards all at once.

I point out that not all Afghans are happy with the occupation forces.

'These people are very few. Most of the people they want,' Mr Airline insists.

'Some of the people I have spoken to are opposed,' I point out.

'If the people they are working with the politics then they would understand that we don't have anything to do to improve our country,' Mr Airline interprets. 'If the people know and have full knowledge of the situation then they would agree. Then they would like because without them the war would be coming again.'

'The people do not want more war,' I explain. 'But they don't like the occupation forces and ask why are these foreigners hiding behind barricades? What are they frightened of? Are they frightened of ordinary people? They ask me why does Karzai have American security, what is wrong with Afghans?'

Anwar is listening intently now.

Scratching his chin in concentration.

'He agrees with something,' says Mr Airline pulling at his tie again. 'He says that you know that these foreign forces coming here in Afghanistan they don't have any knowledge of Afghans or of the Afghan situation. They don't know what to do. He is also not agree with these things, but also, if they will be outside in the city it will be the same situation but…I agree with his point that if they are not here then the fighting it will start again.'

'I know that there is still fighting in certain areas,' I continue, struggling with my English under the translator's influence. 'It is all very complicated but people are feeling frustrated and they ask why, after all these years, why is it still like this? They don't seem to understand that it is going to take a long time.'

'In my opinion, Afghans don't like the foreign military service in Afghanistan,' observes Mr Airline. 'From the revolution, from a long time, they are always against these things, but in this time…you know the time is now different and if they are not here maybe the fighting will start again between these parties because everyone wants to come into power.'

Anwar adds, 'For this purpose, it is the need of Afghanistan that these foreign bases be here for a long time. When the government is settled, we don't now have a powerful central government here, for this purpose it is important that they are here.'

'They will never go,' I observe, forgetting, yet again, to be impartial.

'This will be in the future,' Anwar tells me.

'They will not go.'

'Who knows this?' says Mr Airline. 'Only God knows.'

'They say they will go when everything is settled,' says Anwar, as stubborn as me.

I am more than prepared to argue.

'But Anwar...what were you fighting for?'

'For freedom.'

'Now you have American occupation not freedom,' I emotionally insist. 'You were fighting for your home, your land, your family,' insisting that my vision of the *Mujahideen*, my hero worship of the 'Holy Warriors' was not misplaced. 'Now Anwar, your family is not here, your children are being brought up in London so their ideas are different to yours. Will they ever come back? And...if they do then they will be more Western than Afghan. They will not have any ties to the soil of Afghanistan. You are here alone. So all of this fighting, all of these years, all of this hardship and...and...what?'

This distresses me...let alone him.

He wrings his hands, curls up his legs, tries to disappear, to think, put things in perspective.

'When the Russians took Afghanistan Banafsha then we fight against them,' he tries to explain to me, the interpreter completely forgotten now. 'Then factional fighting. Then *Taliban* came from outside the country. Now my children are in UK, in school, they are studying while we are trying to settle in Afghanistan where school is not completed. When everything is settled then I will bring my family here again and continue with my life. This will be very soon. Inshallah.'

'I hope so Anwar but I am afraid that it may not be so.'

'We hope that it will be soon for all Afghanistan Banafsha. Very soon,' he calms me as Farhad comes in to insist that we eat.

We rise slowly to our feet.

There is a silence.

A sadness.

We all feel it...even Farhad.

– III –

Expecting to have lunch on my own, I was surprised to be called to join the men.

More of them than ever by now.

The television room is bursting at the seams.

Anwar indicates a place on the mattress next to him.

I obediently sit down.

Survey the scene.

The old-fashioned suits, the wide ties, the no-ties, the stack of Kalashnikovs leaning against a mobile gas heater in one corner.

Kebabs, salad, *nan*, Pepsi spread out on the plastic floor cloth.

Discussions in Dari and Pashto.

Farhad rushing in and out, making sure everything is as it should be.

Mr Obeid is informing someone of the merits of Persian poetry.

He asks Anwar to comment.

Anwar grunts.

Being his normal self.

He is lost in thought.

Deeply submerged inside himself.

He picks at his food.

He is completely separate from the others.

He is somewhere else entirely.

'Have some Pepsi,' burps Mr Airline waving a full glass in my direction.

I refuse.

'Oh! I forgot,' he observes in mock surprise, eyebrows raising to merge with his retreating hairline.

'You don't like anything American do you?'

'No,' I reply, asking how they can even consider drinking the stuff.

'Because it's cold and it's easily available,' he tells me, taunting me.

'So is water,' I rise to the bait.

'Some of the things you said in there,' he indicates my room with a nod of his head. 'You know, about Afghan children brought up in UK and then not liking to come back here.'

I wait for him to continue...so does everyone else.

'Well...where we live, all of us here are in the same area of London... it is just like being in Kabul. We speak our own language, have our own shops, restaurants. There are mosques. We live just the same as if we were here so how can this have a bad effect on the children?'

'They don't only speak Dari in school,' I attempt to explain. 'They must also study English and they are exposed to a completely different culture than here. They go to discos, clubs, mix with many other nationalities, other religions and grow to accept a different type of life than they would have in Afghanistan. I am not saying that this is bad...just that they then expect Afghan culture to be different than it really is and that they will find it hard, if not impossible, to settle down back here. They will want things, a way of life that they cannot have. Then they will be disappointed and want to return to their London way of life.'

He disagrees although others see my point.

'If their parents come back then the children must do the same,' he spouts the obvious. 'If we can return and settle down then so can they.'

'But you were born here, grew up here, you understand the situation. Perhaps your children don't.'

'My children were born here too,' he proudly declares. 'They started school here. I stayed in Kabul through the Russian time, through the rocket time, into *Taliban* time. I only left when the *Taliban* assassinated a minister when he was getting a flight at the airport and they shot me too!' he points at his chest. 'I was evacuated to Pakistan for emergency medical treatment. My family came with me and then we took asylum in UK. Now I am thinking that we should come back. Let things settle down some more and then we will see.'

'How old are your children now?' I ask him.

'High school, college,' he answers. 'I can't bring them right now though. First they must finish their studies.'

'By that time they won't want to come back,' I insist.

'The *Khanum* has a point,' Mr Obeid throws in. 'A valid point.'

'You came from UK and you settled in Pakistan. You have adapted to a different culture…so can the children,' Mr Airline continues. 'Could you settle in Kabul, somewhere in Afghanistan.'

'I think so,' I tell him honestly and am immediately inundated with job offers from the strangers sitting around!

I thank them, 'My home and my life is in Pakistan now. My husband and I are happy there.'

Farhad brings a tray of green tea, Naeem a tray of black.

Anwar suddenly grunts.

He has surfaced from inside his head.

'Do you want to continue with the interview now?' he asks much to my astonishment.

'Yes,' not believing my luck.

He grunts in Mr Airline's direction and the three of us, followed by tea, return to where we had left off.

ANWAR

Anwar appears more comfortable now, lounging back against a cushion on the mattress.

His charcoal grey T-shirt, under grey cotton jacket, over light khaki trousers, rides up to expose a hairy roll of flab.

He is quite obviously not as fit as he used to be.

'My father was in the transport business,' he decides to tell me without prompting.

The lunch break gave him pause for thought.

'He had a truck and delivered things, fruit, vegetables, wood, all over Afghanistan and sometimes to Pakistan. I didn't accompany him on any of these trips as I was too busy with school, university, other things. My mother and father both came from Jegdalek.

'I was born the eldest of five sisters and two brothers. One brother took asylum in Toronto, Canada during the fighting time but he is coming back here in a few days,' he beams at me, delighted at the prospect of seeing his brother again.

'We lived in a large house, here in Kabul before the Russians came. I am from a middle class family not a wealthy one. We had a Volkswagen car, a beetle, a yellow one like a frog. I learnt to drive in this. Then I would take my friends to Shomali Plains, to Kargha and sometimes to Jalalabad. In the winter we would spend time in Jalalabad as that is a warm place. In Kabul school is closed in winter. There used to be a lot of snow here when I was young but this is no longer the case.

We had an apple tree in our garden, we kept chickens and sometimes we had a cow for milk,' he revels in happy memories, eyes twinkling, crinkling at the corners.

I try to picture him as a young boy, a young man in school uniform of shirt, trousers, jacket with books under his arm.

I fail miserably.

'All the time sports and study,' he grins impishly, sips at his tea, reaches for another of my cigarettes.

'What about hunting?' I ask him. 'Did you go hunting?'

'Yes,' he laughs in delight as Mr Airline stares at him open-mouthed in astonishment at this utter transformation.

'Only a little though. In the mountains. In *Jihad* time. Not before that. Only in *Jihad* time.'

'What did you hunt?' Mr Airline asks beating me to it.

'*Khargosh*...hares,' Anwar is almost crying with laughter now.

I sense an Afghan joke coming up.

'*Khargosh* with Kalashnikov!' his eyes water, he brushes tears of hilarity away with the back of his hand.

'Kalashnikov bullet is very fast...it goes straight through...just a hole is left.'

We are all laughing now.

He is infectious.

'But I didn't eat them,' Anwar sheepishly admits. 'I gave them to the others.'

'If life had been different, no *Jihad*, then what career would you have chosen?' I ask breaking the moment.

'In this country, before revolution, before Russians come, then when study is finished I would go into government service,' he tells me not yet resorting to the translator.

'My dream was always to live in freedom, not become involved in any political parties, just to be free from everything. To live my life here in the city and be free.'

'Then *Jihad* came and his life suddenly changed and he went to mountain area,' says Mr Airline who can't stand being left out any longer.

'When you were living in Jegdalek, in-between fighting and planning, what did you think of then?'

Instantly serious he replies, 'At that time, fighting against a super power, I thought that we would never get freedom. In my mind I thought that we would all be martyred and that the Russians would win. I really thought that *Mujahideen* would not win. That Russians would win. That we would all die.'

I am shocked. 'I knew you were going to win,' I tell him.

'But I did not,' he admits, ruefully shaking his head. 'At that time also we were thinking of how to sabotage the government. The first step was that sometimes we would block the road from Kabul to Jalalabad. We did this many times when the Russians were trying to transport military equipment to other provinces. Also, a lot of pressure was on me to destroy power stations but I did not do this myself and not my group. The reason why we did not do this was because that is our property, and that if we do succeed in *Jihad* then we will need to use these things again. So we never destroy any government property for this reason. Never. Maybe some other groups did but we didn't. Also, never did I shoot down the rockets to the cities. This killed a lot of people who were not involved in the fighting and also destroyed a lot of properties. I never did that.'

He has given me my cue.

'You say that you stopped fighting when the *Mujahideen* came to Kabul,' I query.

'Yes.'

'Then when Professor Rabbani became Interim President they invited you to take up a ministerial post and you refused. Why?'

'They offered for me to become "Minister for Disabled and Martyrs" but I did not accept as for that purpose there was not any capacity to do something. There was a lot of disabled and people needing help but there was not any budget for this so I did not accept this post.'

'What were you doing in London when you also visited me in Scotland?'

Mr Airline jumps in, 'When he was first time in London he was President of Sports Committee. During Rabbani's time. Official visit.'

'How did you know I was there?' I had been wondering this ever since.

'He had your telephone number,' Mr Airline claims.

'I hadn't given it to him and it was not my number, it was my parents.'

'So he got in touch with your parents and got it from there,' Mr Airline surmises.

'No.'

Anwar laughs to himself. He is giving nothing away.

'In Jegdalek, in 1983, you called a *Jirga* and different area commanders came,' I jog his memory. You were trying to organize *Itehad* but all sources of information claim that *Itehad* was not started or even discussed until 1985 why is this?'

Mr Airline is now back in control. 'From the beginning he start the original unity from commanders in same region and then start to enlarge this unity,' he explains. 'There were some commanders, like Abdul Haq, who were with him on this and we try our best to make a unity and after that we make a council of *Mujahideen*. A *"Shoora".*'

'Why was this not publicized for two more years?'

'At that time things were not good for *Mujahideen* and the press were not interested,' Mr Airline translates looking at me accusingly. 'The *Mujahideen* did not have the capacity to publish such things and depended on the foreign press.'

'I was at this *Jirga* and I wrote about it,' I defend myself. 'The problem was that no one wanted to know. They were just not interested. It made me very angry.'

Anwar nods in agreement. He understands how I feel.

'How did you get organized initially,' I ask Anwar. 'What happened when you first went to see Professor Rabbani with your letter of introduction from Massoud?'

Anwar laughs, chuckles softly to himself, frames his thoughts as Mr Airline pours more tea.

'When he went to Pakistan and was introduced to Professor Rabbani,' Mr Airline relates. 'Before that he thought that these political parties have very good organization and they will train the people and appoint the commanders. He thought these things but when he went there Professor Rabbani told him to take the guns and go and fight! No training! Nothing!'

'So you had to organize yourself?'

'Yes. After that he meet with some other people, some commanders and discussed with them. Then he go to his native area and people, friends, relatives join him and he made military base. There were 1,500 men under his command in Jegdalek when you were there and more came later. He was the leader of all of these and they were divided into different groups. One group was from 50 to 100 people and every 100 people had one commander. Each group was responsible for different places. For their home place because they knew the road, the countryside, the local situation. But all groups, all commanders were responsible to him?'

'Do you still have that pistol Anwar?' I throw in. 'The Russian one?'

He pats his jacket pocket, he knows exactly what I am talking about.

'Tell me how you got that?'

'We shot down a helicopter by stinger missile then I took the pistol from the pilot. He was dead.'

'I heard a different story,' I tell him quietly.

'What?' Mr Airline demanded indignantly while Anwar listens, poised for action.

'I heard that he captured a Russian officer...alive...that he shot him in the head and then took the pistol.'

'No. That is not true Banafsha,' Anwar says staring me straight in the eyes, boring into my head. 'No. he was dead. It was very difficult to capture a Russian alive. We shot down the helicopter. The pilot was dead when the helicopter hit the ground. He was dead when I took the pistol.'

'What really happened when you stoned the spy in the riverbed Anwar?'

He is startled.

Sits up straight.

Spills his tea.

'What do you mean?' he asks after a pregnant pause. 'What spy?'

I tell him.

He listens.

Mr Airline is frozen to his spot.

'I don't remember,' Anwar eventually whispers into the taunt silence. 'I don't remember. You should ask Gul Ruz.'

His phone starts to ring.

The shrill noise piercing the tension.

He looks at it, jumps up and goes to stand by the window where reception is better.

Mr Airline leaves the room hurriedly.

Anwar is watching me, a strange glint in his eyes as he speaks into the phone.

It is my turn to freeze.

He finishes the call with a series of grunts.

'Karzai,' he indicates the phone which is miniaturized by his powerful wrestler's hands.

'He has called for me now but first...I have to attend a meeting...I will see him later...I will see you tomorrow.'

He is gone.

– IV –

Farhad is fed up.

He's had to race around, purchase food, help serve it, hand out cushions and sit outside the door without lunch or even tea.

I just met him in the kitchen where he was cramming cold, congealed, leftover *kebabs* into his mouth with both hands.

'Are any of those other guys worth interviewing?' I asked.

'I don't even know who they are,' he managed to get out in-between chews. 'But I can't leave until they do.'

Mr Obeid is holding court.

Farhad is well and truly stuck.

I could do with getting out of here myself to be honest.

Gul Ruz's son is supposed to be picking me up later but...who knows.

Doves strut hopefully around the lawn.

The strangers finally leave and Farhad has taken the opportunity to go and see if Gul Ruz is home as he can't get through to him on the phone.

If he is home, then Farhad will take me over himself.

The house feels emptier than ever.

I walk around the lawn, stretch my legs, brave the dusty wind.

Notice bullet holes all down one of the boundary walls.

More across the front of the house where they have been roughly plastered over.

What happened and when?

Farhad returns.

He couldn't find Gul Ruz's home, got lost in Microrayon.

His phone rings…panic stations.

His girl's mother.

His girl wasn't feeling well the other night, or yesterday and today her throat swelled up so badly that she can't eat, can't swallow.

They took her to a doctor and now she is being admitted into hospital.

Farhad rushes off to the rescue.

Waliyat Khan is fussing again.

He wants to know why Gul Ruz's 'buccha' hasn't come yet then had me witness him taking tea cups, nuts etc. out of Mr Obeid's room as he doesn't want to be accused of anything. I don't blame him as he probably had a finger pointed in his direction over the camera incident.

He made yet more green tea for me then announced that, as there was no one else around and he was just going to say his prayers in the guardroom and everyone knows when namaz time is, then he should leave his Kalashnikov with me!!!

First time he's done this.

What the hell is in the air other than dust and a Parwan gale rattling doors and windows, shredding the purdah curtains to ribbons?

I asked him about the bullet holes in the walls but either he doesn't know or isn't telling.

Whoops!

I hear shooting in the distance.

Hope it doesn't come any closer and hope it isn't anything serious.

Hope I can remember how to use a Kalashnikov if I have to.

Waliyat Khan came back to see what I want for supper.

I've been picking at the leftover *kebab* too but Waliyat Khan said there was a fly on it so he's thrown it in the bin.

He has insisted on bringing me a yard of hot *nan* and two mangoes on the flowery, plastic lace cloth that is reserved for me.

I was just cutting into a mango when Farhad came rushing in to tell me his girl is back from the hospital after having a drip. That he was just going to drop me off at Gul Ruz's as he now had a guide, that Gul Ruz wanted me to spend the night there but if I didn't want to stay then Khair Muhammad would bring me back later.

Off we go into the wind-ripped darkness.

Farhad driving, his buddy distracting him by pulling semi-precious stone after stone out of his depthless pockets to hold up for examination.

They are trying to start a stone business.

More jiggery pokery.

Up the stairs to Gul Ruz's apartment where Darwish flings open the battered door in delight.

'Banafsha. Banafsha,' he shouts, not in jeans today but a smart *shalwar kameez*, grey on grey, which he wears for school.

He hauled me inside, slammed the door, grabbed my *chappals* and locked them in a wardrobe so that I couldn't leave.

Gul Ruz isn't home, Khair Muhammad was attending to guests.

Darwish dragged me into the family room and Marina, still in black and gold lurex, long curly hair in a flowered scarf, came in from the kitchen, wooden spoon in hand, to give me an exuberant greeting before rushing back to stir her pots and pans, brave the hissing pressure cooker.

Darwish took command in a mixture of Dari, Pashto, Urdu and English, the latter two he learns in school. Not bad for a ten-year-old.

He brought me his school books to see, first in Pashto and Dari, which he proudly read out, then his English book for help with his homework.

No illustrations of bombs, hand grenades and guns as in *Taliban* times but an excellent learner's book printed by Oxford University Press in Pakistan. We started at the front and were working our way through when a thought suddenly struck me. Yes. When I pointed to a word, out of sequence, number five instead of number three, he continued his flow uninterrupted...he is learning by rote!

Dust Motes – 19

Then it was photograph time with Marina rushing in and out still brandishing her wooden spoon, using it to stir the conversation when we got stuck.

She only speaks Dari, my bit of Pashto wasn't much help.

She kept telling me something about a Japanese journalist called Kiko who also went to Jegdalek with the *Mujahideen*.

I eventually fathomed out that Kiko married a relative of Gul Ruz called Dr Talib (Not a *Taliban* as I first thought), in this apartment last year.

Marina explained Kiko's age with fingers and hands.

Expressing her amazement that they should wait until Kiko was 45 years old before getting married and going off to live in Japan.

She is sad that there won't be any children.

Marina is 35, Gul Ruz more than 50, she refused to believe that I am older than Kiko.

From a tattered brown envelope, unearthed from a locked drawer in the ancient desk which the television and video player stand on, a precious hoard of photographs emerged.

All taken after *Taliban* time.

All previous photographs lost between refugee camps, Shomali Plain, Panjshir.

Here was Kiko's wedding, here were the children, three born in Pakistan, three in Panjshir.

Here was a distraught Marina at Gul Ruz's hospital bedside last year after the car crash and fire.

A very strange photograph to treasure.

He with one arm in traction, the other in bandages, his abdomen too.

Her looking wild and wonderful.

Gul Ruz back home and surrounded by children, Marina with her arms around his neck, proudly and defiantly protecting her man.

She would kill for him.

I can see that.

She would fight to the death for him, her children, her home, her country.

She told me how they fled Kabul as the *Taliban* entered.

Leaving with little more than the clothes on their backs, some food wrapped in *chadars*.

The baby tied to her back.

The middle one carried by Gul Ruz.

The eldest, Darwish, tied to her waist with a piece of cloth so that he wouldn't be lost.

The screaming crowds.

Having to abandon the public transport when it ran out of fuel.

The sounds of rockets.

Shooting.

The panic.

Reaching Shomali Plain after hours of walking.

Not knowing about mines.

Sleeping in the open.

Trying to get ahead of the retreating Northern Alliance.

Mujahideen assisting them when they could.

Caught up in the exodus.

Mixed in with fighters in reverse.

Finally finding shelter in a mud brick ruin along with five other families.

Not knowing that this would be home for the next six months.

The desperate searching for food.

The birth of a daughter.

The retreat into a small cave as winter moved in and they moved on to Panjshir itself.

The birth of two more children.

Finally the apprehensive return to Kabul when the American bombing stopped.

She thinks that the Americans are wonderful as they got rid of the *Taliban* and brought peace.

Her Microrayon apartment is a serene heaven.

Her haven.

Her hope for the future.

It is her life.

– V –

She asked me for photographs.

The only one I had with me was of my husband with two of our dogs.

Marina was totally entranced by his long white hair, tied back in a pony tail and her youngest son, Zebiullah was captivated by Bitsy, a brindle cross between a Boxer and a Miniature Dachshund, he commandeered the picture, ran from room to room, showing everyone the 'Tager—Tager' with Darwish in close pursuit yelling 'No. Bitsy— Bitsy and Lucy too.'

The innocent delight of children.

Dinner, which I didn't want, chicken which I don't eat, yards of *nan*, vegetable *pilau*, kidney beans, watermelon, a glass of water which I was wary of until she brought the kettle, demonstrated that the water had been boiled.

Gul Ruz came in, looking exhausted, he'd been at work since 6 a.m. and it was now 9 p.m.

Wearily asked if I had come to do more work.

Relieved when I told him 'No'.

He rolled on the floor with Zebiullah listening to tales of 'Tagers' then went to eat with the guests in the other room.

Eventually Khair Muhammad came, very formally, to take his leave as he was returning to his own home in Bagrami where his mother, his wife, were waiting for him.

Much to Marina's dismay, I requested to be dropped back here, explaining that I didn't know at what time Anwar was coming to be interviewed, maybe 8 a.m., 10 a.m., 12 noon.

One of her daughters, Nadia, who had been showing me pictures of flowers which she collects from chewing gum packets, rushed to rescue my *chappals*.

Darwish was fast asleep.

I went to say farewell to Gul Ruz.

He jumped to his feet.

Put out his hand.

'If you have any more questions you should telephone me Banafsha,' he said.

'Kabul is too dangerous. You should not come back.'

His eyes mirrored his soul as he searched deeply in mine.

I almost choked on the pain, the torture, the feelings I saw there.

'*Khuda Hafiz*,' I whispered.

'*Khuda Hafiz*,' he replied.

He stood and watched me leave.

The same, yet totally different man, who had stood by the big empty bomb in Jegdalek, hand raised in farewell.

Khair Muhammad brought me back here in his Land Cruiser of all things.

He had been to school in Haripur with Waliyat Khan, classmates, so they stood and chatted a while at the gate until the arrival of a second Land Cruiser, dusty, dented, bearing the legend 'Sarobi Police', pulled in.

'Friends,' said Waliyat Kan. 'No problem. Friends.

I was just falling asleep at 11:30 p.m. when I came to with a jump.

The whole house was shaking and the noise, a roll of thunder combined with an earthquake, sent my blood pressure pulsating through the roof.

An armed convoy rolling past.

Helicopters overhead.

The occupation forces are menacing.

I don't like it at all.

END OF PART SEVEN

PART EIGHT

– I –

Up bright and early for another cold shower.

Finally got the hang of the *chula*.

One knob and three hot plates so you need to move the knob around as required and get it on at the right angle with just the right amount of force to make it work.

Mr Obeid surfaced as I was drinking my second cup of coffee, asking if I had put the metal bucket of water on the *chula* to heat.

Not me.

Farhad had come back and it was his.

His girl is okay now but his throat is giving a problem.

Hope I don't get whatever it is.

'Sabir is bringing me a dog today,' he tells me, happy at the prospect of canine company.

He doesn't know what kind of dog only that 'It's a good one'

Mr Airline arrived, departed.

Mr Obeid left too.

Farhad has gone to find a pharmacy, get something for his throat.

Naeem is watering the lawn.

Waliyat Khan is oiling his Kalashnikov in his usual spot by the gate.

I…also as usual…am waiting for Anwar.

A creased, crumpled, unshaven, rather unsavoury man in a baggy grown suit wandered in looking for Anwar.

From London, a taxi here from the airport.

Expected to meet Anwar here.

No one knows where he is.

Farhad came back, explained that he would have to take the new arrival on an Anwar hunt and I haven't seen them since.

Lunch time comes and goes.

Fried eggs, tomatoes and *nan*.

I sit on my mattress and curse.

Sit on my mattress and travel back through time.

To yet another place of waiting.

– II –

Teramangal on the Pakistan side of the Afghan border.

Sitting on a pile of fragrant, rough cut cedar.

Gunshots, machine-gun fire fragmenting the fresh mountain air.

An outlaw town of tents, mud huts and shanties.

Mujahideen preparing to cross the border and fight.

Others returning.

Refugees.

Camels, horses, cows, herds of sheep and goats.

Hidden in a black *chadar* waiting for Anwar to complete organizing the journey to war.

Engineer Namak.

Shifty grey eyes and a pointed nose.

Going on *Jihad* for the first time.

Wearing *shalwar kameez*, a *chadar*, plastic sandals...nothing else, no other luggage...no gun.

An English speaker.

Offering a handful of green grapes.

Washing them in filthy water in an empty motor oil tin whilst warning of cholera.

Even a woman in a *chadar* attracted too much attention.

Taken down through a crowded alley into a tiny, narrow shop built of wood.

A money changer at the front, gun shop in the back.

Commander Anwar deep in negotiations with both.

Given a plate of rice, a teaspoon to eat with.

A glass of water, more grapes.

The waiting endless.

Negotiations continuing.

Peering at the outside world through a small hole in the wood work.

Taking in details of different tribal features, clothes, decorated guns, turbans, hats, plastic shoes, car tire sandals, leather boots.

Eating lunch whilst sitting on a box of mines.

Suddenly realizing that a pair of leather knee boots, shined to a gloss finish, had stopped, walked on, returned, stopped again.

Eyes travelling upwards from the boots to snow white jodhpurs, immaculate white, short *kameez*, intricately embroidered waistcoat, crossed bandoliers of bullets, an ornate shotgun across one shoulder and pistol in a leather holster at his waist.

A hawk nosed, arrogant face, luminous grey eyes, moustache, spotless white turban with a tail of cloth draped down his back.

Absolutely stunning.

Eyes met eyes.

Quickly pulling the black *chadar* close but...too late.

He called to Gul Ruz who took in the situation at a glance.

Ordered into the very back of the shop while they argued...
furiously.

The apparition had tried to buy me.

Such things come out of having to wait endlessly in the strangest of
locations imaginable.

Commander Anwar reappearing after a long absence.

He had been trying to hire a horse for the journey ahead but found
them too expensive.

40,000–50,000 Afghanis.

'You can walk?'

'Yes.'

Sitting on a box of hand grenades and waiting to go and face the
Soviet war machine with a group of *Mujahideen* in whose hands I was
placing my life.

Always the waiting...followed...at some eventual point...by the
inevitable rush.

This seems to be a particularly Afghan code.

– III –

7 p.m. The day crawls towards an empty close.

It takes thirty-three paces to cross the patio and almost an hour to
complete 2,222 slow paces, cursing all the time, around the lawn.

I counted every single step...bored and angry.

Dust Motes – 18

Mr Obeid came back pulling his hair out although his reasons are
different.

I make tea and he pours out his problems as we drink it.

'I met with Karzai,' he fumes.

'He wants to give me an important position and I do want to do something for my country but I am so angry, frustrated with everything that is, or isn't, going on,' he repeatedly runs the fingers of both hands through his hair, almost dragging it out by the roots as he sounds off.

'I am thinking of dividing my time between UK and Afghanistan as my wife, who is a lawyer, refuses to come back here. She absolutely refuses, says there is nothing here to come back to and no proper education for our son. She can't manage without me. She just can't do things. She phoned and told me her car is due for its MOT and Road Tax and she needs me to do it. She banged the car and needs me to sort that out too.'

Surely, in his position, he has someone to do these things for him.

'My son phoned asking me to come home,' he continues, eyes blazing, voice full of raw emotion. 'He's only five years old. He was crying. I told him that he is a man now, that he must be brave but had a hard job convincing him of this.'

I imagine that his wife dialed the number, putting on the pressure.

'If I do come here then I told Karzai that I will need a decent house, twenty-four hour electricity, hot water.'

I suppose that millionaires don't have to heat bathwater in a tin bucket on a *chula*!

'I would need to have servants, a decent cook, a proper vehicle etc. etc. I think my wife is worried that if I move here alone that I might take a second wife but still, she won't come. Kabul stinks and it's filthy but I still want to come. I really don't know what to do.'

Yes. Some parts of the city do smell but it is very clean compared to some of the villages, towns and cities in Pakistan.

He has been in UK too long and not taken a walk through a slum area there either.

'Are you being eaten alive at night?' he asks. 'I can't sleep for things biting me. I'm covered in itchy bumps from head to toe.'

I haven't been bitten at all.

I give him an antihistamine and suggest he sends Naeem for bug spray.

He does and uses up the entire can.

The fumes are suffocating even in here.

He has gone to dinner with some former Army General who opposes Karzai.

Playing both ends against the middle I presume.

Before he left though, he phoned Anwar.

'The *Khanum* is very angry,' he told him.

Anwar says he will come in the morning before I leave for the airport.

We will continue the interview then.

– IV –

Farhad races in.

He is cursing too.

The Parwan Wind is enjoying tormenting people today.

His girl is very sick again, he has to take her back to the hospital.

He got commandeered by Anwar whose driver has disappeared.

'Karzai called him and I had to drive him there,' he rants. 'Then, for security, me and his guards had to wait in the Pajero for four f... hours!!! And, as soon as he came out he got called to a funeral and then to settle a land dispute. When he arrived there I got the call telling me about my fiancé so I left him, came here to pick up some stuff now I have to go again. Sorry about this Banafsha.'

He is gone again.

A tall, slim, confused London kid in a heavy, black leather jacket, T-shirt, jeans, sneakers.

I wonder which planet he inhabits.

Certainly a very different one than mine.

– V –

Anwar is working on *Itehad* again and has been for over a year.

Trying to forge alliances, allegiances among warlords, former enemies, two-faced side switchers like Dostum.

I don't understand how he can bear to be in the same room with them let alone hold negotiations.

I would not be able to do this.

That much I know.

He considers this to be necessary.

A move that without which there cannot be any form of lasting peace.

It is necessary to forget the past, put it away, store it in a safe place and move forwards.

There is a future to construct, to be built on the bitter ashes of the past.

So bitter that even I can taste them.

He is playing a leading role in this process.

It has not yet been reported in the press.

Is he putting me on the spot again I wonder?

Jegdalek in 1983.

Anwar organizing *Itehad* then.

The bombed out village, 6,000 feet above sea level, 60 miles from the Pakistan border, 30 miles from Kabul.

Invigorating mountain air.

60 miles behind enemy lines.

Wrapped in a black *chadar* beneath my '*Gun Tree*'.

Listening to the rhythm of morning.

A hand-written note arrives from Anwar, is duly translated, instructions issued.

Escorted by my bodyguards to a meeting at some other place.

Walking, in silence, up the dry river bed.

9 a.m. and the sky is full of Soviet planes.

Helicopters.

Sheltering beneath dusty trees until they move on.

Jet engines, rotor blades moving away.

Coming back.

Going away again.

A different mountain.

A different camp.

Three anti-aircraft guns dug into the slippery scree mountainside.

One large bomb shelter, a second, designed by Namak who was a civil engineer in Kabul before the war, being excavated by a group of *Mujahideen*.

I am taken into the first bomb shelter.

Told to sit.

The anti-aircraft guns spring into action.

I freeze.

A false alarm.

The bomb shelter didn't appear to be very strong.

Visions of being buried alive.

Posters in Pashto and Dari on the walls.

Religious artifacts, lucky charms made from brightly coloured wool and cloth, bundles of belongings, the inevitable guns hanging from thick, wooden roof beams.

The walls and floor are solid rock.

Someone brought a plate of unripe, green peaches, green walnuts and tea.

I rose, looked out of the entrance and was shocked to see my blue sleeping bag on my rooftop, far away in the distance yet perfectly clear.

If I could see it then so could the helicopters.

I must hide it away in the future...if there is one.

My guards, Mirwais and Faizullah, argue over who should carry the Chinese sub-machine gun and who the vintage Lee-Enfield rifle.

Mirwais wins.

A group of *Mujahideen* accompanied by a *mullah* enter and sit around the walls.

I sat cross-legged in baggy olive green army trousers, loose grey shirt, *chadar* by my side.

My *chappals* left at the entrance as is customary.

Namak suddenly suggest that I cover my feet with my *chadar* as this would be 'far more polite'.

Everyone else had bare feet so I didn't understand the problem but complied.

'It would be better if you raise it to cover your knees too,' Namak suggested, miming the action.

My surprise showed.

'In our country even men do not sit like that, they cover themselves, so even though nothing is happening it is better that no one sees.'

Realizing what he was alluding too, I almost died of shame, scribbling in my notebook in a vain attempt at disguising my embarrassment.

'Are you writing about the covering process?' Namak asked.

I could have strangled him on the spot!

ANWAR

The heavy mob arrive.

Anwar, Gul Ruz and a group of strange commanders one of whom resembles a bear.

A very large man, huge jaw, black hair and beard, very deep-set, darting eyes, huge white teeth like piano keys, the apparition topped by a *pakol* hat worn at a very jaunty angle.

He had a strange, to me, way of smoking.

Holding the cigarette in a huge, clenched paw, sucking the smoke through his fist with an extremely loud intake of breath and coughing every time.

These seven commanders and the *mullah*, arranged themselves in a half circle in the centre of the bomb shelter.

Everyone else, including Namak the interpreter, were sent out.

I stayed where I was.

The *mullah* lead them all in prayers.

I watched, listened.

After prayers a pile of papers were passed around.

These were powerful leaders, not ordinary guys, something was definitely going on.

Letters passed around, discussions going on.

A pile of official looking documents all signed and countersigned by the seven commanders.

Anwar signing each document, possibly twice.

Signing concluded, more prayers, then three bundles were placed in a pile, the Holy Quran on top.

They took some kind of solemn oath, touched their lips and foreheads to the Holy Quran.

Rose to their feet, filed out in dignified majesty.

I had absolutely no idea what I had just witnessed.

Anwar returned, called Namak to explain.

'This meeting was a *"Jirga"* which is a "grand council" and Commander Anwar was the President of this session,' he importantly translated.

'This *Jirga* was to discuss unity between different parties of *Mujahideen*. This movement is called *"Itehad"*. The commanders who were here have agreed to co-operate in all matters such as sharing their ammunition, money and everything. All future operations and decisions relating to these groups in this area will be discussed by the *Jirga*. They want to spread unity throughout Afghanistan. This *Jirga* is an important step to achieving the ultimate goal of unity for *Mujahideen* all over the country. By combining all *Mujahideen*, all resources, we will become strong and evict the Russians from Afghanistan.'

'Please explain the primary purpose of this unity?' I ask Anwar, still not realizing the historic moment I had been allowed to witness.

'The purpose is to put more pressure on the enemy and free Afghanistan. No other purpose,' he tells me. 'After the Russians leave, there will be central unity in Kabul and this unity will be continued to create a struggle for a pure Islamic Government.'

'Is a government including non-Islamic parties acceptable?' I probe.

'No,' is Anwar's instant response. 'They will not allow other political groups to be active. There are two at the moment, one is the "Afghan Millat" who wish to split up Afghanistan and the other is the "Sholo group" who are supported by Chinese Maoists and the people will not be deceived by communists again.'

'Why are the *Mujahideen* so determined to overcome the Russians who vastly outnumber and out power them?'

'Old history of Afghanistan from the beginning is that they have never allowed foreign intervention,' Anwar proudly declares. 'And, being Muslims, they have always fought and died obtaining benefit from God and stay in Paradise for ever, and at the same time,' he grins mischievously, 'If they beat the enemy....that is also good.'

The *mullah*, who returned in time to hear this interchange, explained, 'A Muslim *Mujahideen* who dies fighting goes directly to Paradise. Other Muslims, not *Mujahideen*, also go to Paradise but only after some interrogation!'

I smile at the translation.

'What particular items do the *Mujahideen* need?' I ask Anwar.

He jumps on this question angrily.

'Why? Why does she want to know? Can you help us or are you going to tell the world our weak points?'

Anwar and the *mullah* argue for sometime.

Eventually he admits that their prime needs are food, clothing, ammunition, mine detectors, communication and decoding machines along with, of all things, inflatable boats!

The meeting is over.

I wonder how to help.

We return to our camp.

Dodging helicopters, spotter planes on the way.

The *Mujahideen* play volleyball in the evening.

I really don't understand them at all.

Nothing has changed.

So, Anwar is organizing *Itehad* again.

I wonder what lessons he learnt from his previous experience.

– VI –

The Parwan Wind is furious tonight.

It rips the darkness apart.

It is banging the windows, doors, clanking the entrance gates.

It is impossible to tell if anyone is coming in, going out.

I lie on my mattress in the grey dark...not on a roof top this time, feeling under house arrest.

My last night in Afghanistan...again.

It is almost impossible to sleep.

Impossible to anchor myself in the current reality.

To put the pieces together.

The wind won't allow me to even think clearly.

If it doesn't calm down...I think I may go insane.

As the hurricane of jumbled up thoughts, images, bounces around inside my bursting skull a deafening storm of gunshots kicks me back to exactly where I started out.

Afghanistan.

A country of confusions.

END OF PART EIGHT

PART NINE

– I –

5 a.m., and I am already on the prowl.

Too keyed up to sleep.

The cement mixers, not a water pump, have already started up next door.

Reconstruction.

The noise and dust fill my ears, my eyes, my mouth.

I close the windows in a vain attempt at blotting things out.

It doesn't work.

A leisurely cold shower at 7 a.m. to shock me awake, jolt my brain into action.

Cleanse the atmosphere, put order into the chaos inside my skull.

The door handle rattles desperately.

Mr Obeid...stomach out, throat sore, sinus problem, chest infection, the works.

Farhad rushes in at 7:30 a.m. all in a fluster.

'Are you ready Banafsha?'

'Ready for what?'

'You have to be at the airport at 9 a.m. don't you, so Anwar is just coming.'

'No. 2 p.m.' I tell him, quickly adding, 'But don't tell Anwar or he may not show up at all.'

He tells him anyway.

9 a.m., packed and waiting.

Dressed in my 'Meet the President' outfit for good luck.

Mr Airline arrived a little while ago.

A navy blue tie today.

Keyed up to translate.

Raring to go.

Farhad is feeling better today but complains that the doctor made him have an injection then wanted to give him a drip.

He refused.

First time he's been to a doctor here and did not enjoy the experience.

The doctor sounds as if he trained in Pakistan where people tend to think that they haven't been treated correctly unless they get an injection, a drip and a handful of 'golis'.

Farhat displays two strips of 'golis' and another of Panadol CF.

'London doctors are better,' he grumbles. 'More with it you know.'

I think of the 'wedding doctor' and his fixed grin.

Of his eldest daughter who wants to become a doctor, marry a doctor.

She had worn a Rs 5,000 boutique outfit, purchased in Peshawar, for the event and had recently spent Rs 15,000 on having a Kuchi outfit stitched by a tailor here.

'I will be a doctor,' she confided. 'Then I will marry a doctor. He must be tall and fair if possible. Then we will go and have a free life in America. Better still, I will marry an Afghan doctor who already has American nationality. I do not intend to have any children though and he will have to agree to this condition. Neither will I permit him to take a second wife in order to have children by her. No children. We will just be doctors not parents. We will be free.'

She wants the world, a husband, on her terms.

I doubt she will get her wish.

10:10 a.m. Anwar and bodyguards arrive in a dusty, dark blue Toyota Corolla.

He is ensconced with Mr Airline and a bunch of strangers in the other room.

Naeem wanders around with plates of mangoes, pots of tea.

Farhad paces up and down.

A cat on hot bricks.

I wonder what is eating him?

Finally, 10:45 a.m. Anwar comes to continue the interview.

'I can only stay until 11:30 a.m.,' he tells me with a hint of his old, mischievous grin. 'I have a meeting with President Karzai scheduled for 12 o'clock.'

There is no mention of the meeting he was supposed to arrange for me.

I briefly wonder if I could possibly tag along. I am dressed for the occasion after all.

He sees me framing the request.

Smiles, shakes his head.

I don't voice my thoughts.

He is dressed in light olive green trousers today, a pastel coloured, open neck shirt, a light brown suede jacket with a designer label.

Smart yet casual.

I suppose you must be at least smart when going to meet your president.

Mr Airline takes his place on the floor.

Anwar on the end of my mattress.

He lounges back, helps himself to my cigarettes and we begin... again.

ANWAR

My time is fast running out so I get straight to the point.

'Were you with the Northern Alliance Anwar?'

'There was no Northern Alliance after *Taliban* is finished, gone,' translates Mr Airline as Anwar's eyes spark into sudden wariness.

'Yes. I know this,' I tell him, watching Anwar. 'But I want to know about the time before this. When the Northern Alliance was active.'

'When Massoud was alive then I was with him. Always I was with him.' He skirts the question, wary of thin ice.

'I was with him against *Taliban* and we tried to remove them and for that purpose we had some meetings, like those in Bonn, Istanbul, some other places, aimed at removing the *Taliban* as this was the only way it could be done.'

Massoud was not in Bonn or Istanbul.

Anwar was not with him all of the time.

He was not fighting on the front line with Gul Ruz all the time.

He was partly with his family in London, partly attending political meetings in Europe.

How did he travel there and who footed the bill?

'Sometimes I was with Northern Alliance,' he defends himself. 'After *Taliban* is finished, then we came to Kabul and took over, then Northern Alliance is finished in my opinion.'

He is distancing himself from the atrocities they are reported to have committed.

I don't blame him at all.

He is sitting up straight, tense, paying full attention.

I change direction again.

'What happened when you were injured by shrapnel back in 1983?'

'This was in action between *Mujahideen* and Russians.'

Mr Airline is all ears.

He is enjoying himself now.

'It happened in Sarobi district. He took a mortar shell in his hip and back. He still has some piece inside his body. The doctors say it is too near his kidney to remove,' he tells me, revelling in the details.

'Do you miss your days in the mountains Anwar? The brotherhood? The camaraderie?'

'Those days were very difficult and very hard, especially for me as the commander,' he tells me directly, relaxing back against the cushions again, reminiscing. 'If I explained these difficult days in full, then no one would ever believe what it was really like. Those were the days of starting the revolution against the Russians, against the communist parties. That time was the voice of freedom.'

'The other day you said you would think of some incidents, stories about Jegdalek to tell me. Have you done this?'

He nods, smiles briefly, calls for black tea.

'A nice and lovely day was that when there was no bombardment from Russians, from government to us.'

I acknowledge this.

I shared this experience.

It haunts me still.

Every time I hear a helicopter…no matter where I am…I am back in Jegdalek hiding under '*The Gun Tree*'.

Waiting to see if it flies over…bombs us or not.

'On these days we could play volleyball.'

He knows I recall this too.

I still have the photographs though I need no reminder.

'Still,' he continues sipping the scalding tea which Naeem has quickly produced. 'Those were difficult days. It was a very difficult time. It was not easy to be a *Mujahideen* Commander. I lost so many good friends, close friends, nice boys, *Mujahids*.

So many people are not with us in this world now.'

He stares into a space only he can see, 'The people who live in these mountain areas...they are believers...they love us,' he states simply whilst I wonder just how many of the people he speaks of now feel betrayed.

Feel bitter about what happened when the *Mujahideen* marched into Kabul, the terrible bloodbath which followed, the horrors that also plagued the footsteps of the Northern Alliance.

The uneasy peace they live with.

The new foreign occupation they must endure.

Love is so close to hate at the best of times and this is certainly not one of them.

'I heard how Waliyat Khan's elder brother and a friend of his used to have competitions,' I said. 'That when a Russian convoy travelled along the Jalalabad highway they would each grab grenades and try to out run each other, see who could reach the Russians first.'

He nods, smiles sombrely, 'This is true. They are both dead now.'

I speak into the silence which threatens to engulf us.

'Have you remembered who that *Maulvi* was?'

'No Banafsha. I don't remember. I never kept any notes of that time. Now a lot of people are writing about *Mujahideen* time and when we read it, we see it is not true because we were there and they were not. Some of them are writing from their own ideas.'

'That's because you won't tell us what really happened.' I defend my trade.

He is suddenly serious.

He puts down his cup, leans forwards, clasping his knees.

'One story they tell is that when the *Mujahideen* took over Kabul... there is one police station...' He pauses, concentrates, chews on his lower lip. 'What they say is not true.'

'What police station Anwar? What do they say?'

'One story they say, say that it is true, is that it was told by Shia people who live in that area called Chendaul, that *Mujahideen* took over that police station when they came to Kabul but that is not true. The true story is that there was this one *Mujahid*, a brother-in-law to Massoud, he came to Kabul and had some *Mujahideen* with him and they took over that police station.'

He is confusing me.

I cannot make sense of what he says.

'I don't understand Anwar.'

He has thunderclouds in his eyes, he is highly agitated, extremely upset.

He tries again.

'What happened with this police station is before take over of Kabul city. The attack was only just starting on Kabul city. This was during Amin's time, right at the beginning.'

He is talking of an event that must have occurred back in 1979 when Amin and Taraki, both leftist leaders, were engaged in a vicious power struggle, a struggle which Amin briefly won, an event for which he was soon assassinated.

Whatever happened at this police station happened in 1979 and not when the *Mujahideen* took Kabul in 1992.

An event replayed out of context, out of time.

He will not elaborate.

I have not yet been able to locate a source of information.

I still do not know the full story.

I took the opportunity, 'After the *Mujahideen* took over Kabul then a lot of very bad news reports were given. I don't know what is true and what is not.'

'I think that some of the bad things they did happen,' he sadly admits without going any further.

His face is full of ghosts, images, pictures he will not share.

He is the one who has to live with them and he does not want to resurrect them now.

Least of all to me.

Thoughtfully he continues, 'In the beginning the *Mujahideen* had a very good and very close relationship with the people. With the people in the villages, in the provinces, in the mountain areas. We were all in this together. All of them believed each other. They had a very good relationship. This was very necessary in guerrilla warfare. It is like if you take a fish out of water then it cannot survive and it was same for *Mujahideen* who depended on the people. They were also together like the fish and the water. But when they took over Kabul, when *Mujahideen* took over Kabul and *Mujahideen* were in power, there is some mischief from *Mujahideen* leaders. They make some relationships, some contacts with communist peoples, especially with members of the Intelligence Service which was under the guidance of the Russians here, then they mixed with these and did not do the things that would be good for all the people. They made mistakes and they made mischief.'

The bubble burst.

The dream ruptured.

Twisted ambitions, reality crept in through the door which was supposed to have opened on freedom.

'How do you feel when you have to meet with these same people now? People like Dostum?'

'You know Banafsha, that time has now come to an end. We have to put these things behind us. But, we have an idea in our minds as to who will destroy this country and who will be right but this is not the time to discuss these things. *Jihad* time was a clean and nice time. At that time we fought to take over Afghanistan, to push the Russians out of the country. That was the main thing during that time. In this time now we do not have any other way because if we will not discuss the things with these people then the fighting will come again. Again there will be problems for the people. The country will be destroyed.

'We are starting the rehabilitation of the country. We are working towards the time that everybody will shake hands and we will start to rebuild the country again.'

'How do you see your own future position in this?'

'I am not clear about a government position. That it is small or that it is big. I am not going through that because I don't have any interest in these things. The only thing is that I am trying to make a unity between ethnic groups in Afghanistan. To get them all to work together and rebuild Afghanistan. Now I am concentrating on trying to do these things.'

'How is this progressing?'

'We are progressing well.'

'How long before anything positive comes about?'

'When *Taliban* is gone,' Anwar explained. 'When Karzai comes in…one group…that is Northern Alliance comes to Kabul. Karzai's people come to Kabul. People from Kandahar. People returning from European countries. In the beginning there was very small mistakes between each other in Kabul city, in government, in some positions. Then there were complaints to Karzai and Karzai, he was busy with these things, but from that day, we start to negotiate about that with each other. Now this thing is finished in Kabul. Now we want to extend these things into the provinces outside Kabul. Now this is going on. It is difficult. That is true. Very difficult things.'

He leans forwards, speaking softly, almost conspiratorially.

'One other thing is that Afghanistan has some enemies outside the country. Some other countries, I will not name them, they do not want unity inside Afghanistan.'

He does not mention Pakistan.

He is being diplomatic.

I know he includes my country in his list.

He knows that I know.

It remains an unspoken understanding between us.

'Despite all of this, we are trying our best but we really don't have enough of budget for all of this. We do not have enough of budget to enlarge these things to outside of the capital limits.'

He sighs, deeply, spreads his hands in a gesture of resignation. 'Anyway...we are trying our best to do something.'

'Do you feel that Karzai is strong enough to achieve these things Anwar?'

'Karzai's position gets stronger day by day,' he insists. 'From the beginning, when Karzai came to power, the situation is very changed and he is more in power in this day. Now he is in a good position.'

I dispute this strongly.

'But he is still hiding behind American security and barbed wire. If he came out and met with the people, if they could see him as a strong person, would that not help? In the Sultanate of Oman...when there is a problem in the south, Sultan Qaboos goes there, he sits in *jirga* with the people, talks with them, eats with them and they respect him for this. Respect him for not showing fear.'

He ponders this, rolling the concept around inside his head, habitually chewing his plump bottom lip again.

He gives a typical Anwar style grunt.

Reaches for his lukewarm tea.

Finally speaks.

'Afghanistan is in a different position than other countries because in Afghanistan now the long time war is finished. During war this Al-Qaeda people's centre was here as you know. The other thing is that Afghanistan has foreign enemies. These are trying to do something. Mr Karzai is not afraid of Afghans...it is from outsiders who will do things from inside a crowd of Afghans. For this purpose, for a short time, there is need of foreign security.'

'What do you advise Mr Karzai on Anwar?' I ask. Cheekily adding, 'I'm sure it isn't just sports!'

His private mobile phone rings shrilly, interrupting the flow.

Anwar looks at the number, smiles to himself, looks at me then turns his face away, mutters something unintelligible to the caller, turns back with a grin.

I repeat my question as his mind is now elsewhere.

He is in another dimension.

I tread warily.

'If you don't want to discuss this then I understand.'

'Mr Karzai,' he starts, nodding respectfully towards the phone clutched in his fist. 'Mr Karzai has many advisors. They discuss many things. I am also saying things to him about the unity of Afghanistan.'

I note the use of the word 'also'.

He is involved in other things but has lightly skipped the question.

Mr Airline knows this too and looks searchingly at Anwar before telling me, 'He is trying very hard for unity in Afghanistan.'

'So this is the main subject?'

'Yes,' they both immediately agree.

I am not going to be told more and I know it.

The finality in their voices is loud and clear.

Whatever Anwar is really doing is absolutely none of my business.

'How many years were you in London and how did you spend your time there?' I go back to this as I still sense gaps, gaps in time which remain black holes to me.

'I was not being permanently in London,' he replies rather hesitantly, testing the waters before committing himself further.

'I was just in and out for a short time.'

'What did you do when you were there?' I ask, knowing that he would have done far more than simply spent the time with his family, knowing that he is not that type of person, knowing that his mould is of a political bent.

'When Hekmatyar was firing rockets into Kabul that was very bad for us, for Afghanistan,' he tells me, coming from an angle which I can't yet fathom.

'Then, when *Taliban* take over the country and we had to go out of Afghanistan to European country that was a very hard time for me.' He then explains, 'I was in Afghanistan, and in Kabul, through all the fighting times and when we had to leave, then in my mind was only the question of when could we go back to our country. Outside time was not a relaxed time for me.'

I try to picture him in his London home.

Imagine him playing with his children, helping them with homework, kicking a football in the park but see, instead, a vision of a man, shoulders hunched against the damp and rain, walking, alone, along a misty river bank, miserably alone in a crowded street.

A defeated *Mujahideen* commander who cannot exist in limbo.

A man who watches, listens in silence at international conferences which have taken the place of guerrilla warfare.

A person who will not let his world disintegrate but who must try and pull in the remaining fragile threads, haul in the net of survival, harvest whatever crop there is to reap.

I see a patriot.

A patriot who, like the fish and the water, cannot breathe any air except that of his own country.

He is Afghan to the core.

I have asked him before but I find myself asking again, 'Are you happy now Anwar, happy inside yourself?'

He searches his soul, searches his reflection in my concerned eyes.

'No. Not totally Banafsha,' being cruelly honest with himself, with me. 'But we are trying our best that peace will come totally to Afghanistan and that Afghan refugees, all those who have left, will come home.'

'I don't think they will all come back Anwar, particularly those who have gone to places like America. Some will come but many won't return now. The time has been too long.'

He nods in sad agreement, searches for a reason that he can relate to.

Finds one.

'The problem is with children in school. With students. They cannot leave in the middle of studies. It is for that purpose these Afghans are waiting there.'

This is untrue.

The three of us sitting there know it.

I point out a missing generation.

'There is a big gap now Anwar. You are sitting here in Kabul, in Afghanistan, but the next generation, needed to go into government for example…they are not here. Where are you going to find them?'

His sadness is a palpable thing.

Its tortured pulse screams in anguish along with the wind raging through the world outside the closed confines of the room.

'That gap is felt,' he finally concedes. 'These people are studying in the European way. We cannot fill that gap with these people.'

I feel his pain.

He is including his own children in this.

The children of people like Mr Airline, Mr Obeid and so many like them.

He teeters on the precarious edge of a highly personal, highly emotional void.

He appears close to tears.

So am I.

He takes a deep breath, shudders, visibly pulling himself back from the brink.

'But we can fill it with the people who are here. Those getting their education here. They are learning in the true racial, cultural manner and eventually...slowly, slowly...they will come into government here. It will all take time.'

His phone breaks the spell which has woven its silken cobwebs around us.

Startles us with its demanding shrillness.

He looks at it as if it isn't supposed to be there.

Reads the caller's number to himself.

Checks his watch.

Rises, walks to the opposite end of the room to answer.

Karzai is getting impatient.

He indicates that Mr Airline should leave the room.

Puts his phone away and crosses to where I now stand by the window.

'So Banafsha,' he says. 'So now I have to leave.'

I nod mutely.

I hate partings.

I am not very good at them.

'You are leaving too,' a statement not a question. 'But you will come back again I hope. Next time I will be a better host!'

I don't know what to say.

He crosses the space between us.

Begins a farewell handshake.

Changes his mind.

Envelops me in a powerful bear hug.

Whispers something in my ear and is gone.

The true spirit of Afghanistan.

Gone to meet his destiny.

Emotion threatens to choke me.

Rivers of tears scald my face.

I don't know why.

Mr Obeid comes in through the still open door.

Is horrified to find me crying.

'What happened?' He demands. 'Did something happen?'

He looks in the direction of Anwar's departure. 'Did…'

'No. No. Nothing happened,' I reassure him. 'It's just that I don't want to leave. Nothing else.'

'You really love this country don't you,' he says in surprise.

'Yes,' I agree.

'When I build my house here you must come back and design the garden.'

I smile through my still rolling tears.

We shake hands.

He departs.

Mr Airline comes in.

Understands the situation at a glance.

Shakes my hand and is gone.

It is Farhad's turn.

'I have to take them somewhere Banafsha,' he tells me. 'I'll be back in plenty of time to take you to the airport though. Don't worry and please don't cry.'

'I'm okay Farhad. I just hate goodbyes…especially in Afghanistan.'

'You are an Afghan inside,' he says. 'That is the reason,'

Then he is gone too.

END OF PART NINE

EPILOGUE

– I –

Waiting to leave.

Return to my life in Pakistan.

Farhad rushes in once more.

'Sorry about this Banafsha,' he stutters, out of breath.

'I dropped those guys at the Continental Hotel. Now I have to go and pick up a guy who has just arrived from London. I won't be able to take you to the airport after all but everything is arranged and my cousin will take you there. Don't worry.'

I'm not worried.

I'm weary and will take a cab if I have too.

In my mind I have already departed.

A plumpish, smiling, grey-eyed man dressed in a green Afghan Police uniform came to say hello.

'Do you remember me?' he asked with a shy grin.

I don't but have learnt that it is of great importance to people such as this one that I do know who they are.

'Jegdalek,' I reply.

'Of course,' he beams. 'I was with Karimullah. We lead your horse into Jegdalek on the day you arrived.'

We shake hands.

He departs happily.

I am taken, drifting dreamlike, not really present in either body or mind, to the airport in a battered Sarobi Police Hilux.

A criminal being deported.

I find that I don't care.

The driver, a thin man with a thin beard remembers me from Jegdalek too.

'I keep my family in Rawalpindi,' he tells me. 'It is safer for now.'

They deposit me in the VIP lounge.

Return moments later.

Bundle me back inside their vehicle.

Drive out onto the tarmac where a plane is getting ready for departure.

I am half way up the steps before I realize that the plane is the wrong colour.

This is not my PIA flight at all.

A flight to Moscow and I almost went.

They take me back to the terminal and I join the rest of the herd.

I float through the extremely lax security.

Rough looking female staff with too much lipstick and no manners confiscate my lighter, matches, try to steal my makeup.

Now I feel angry, on the defensive.

The departure lounge is bursting at the seams with Russians.

Afghans interacting with them pleasantly.

I can't.

My memories are too deeply etched for that.

Unlike Anwar I can't relate to members of a former enemy race on friendly terms.

It would seem that I am more narrow-minded than I would ever have thought possible.

I feel like an alien.

The Malaysian cooking programme booming out from the wall-mounted television set adds to my inner confusion.

This Afghanistan is not my place.

I am going home.

Travelling back to my mountain retreat to think.

Try to put things into perspective.

Work out what my journey was all about.

I am not absolutely certain that I even want to know.

Dust Motes – 20

Bombed into being in Afghanistan at the age of 27, the woman, clad in *shalwar kameez*, head wrapped in an antique pink shaded shawl, weeps silently in the window seat she has selected.

There are only seven passengers on the flight from Kabul to Islamabad.

She is politely ignored.

Her gaze is fixed on the magnificent mountainscape far below.

Jagged pinnacles, a turquoise blue lake, glistening snow.

The desolation of arid plains provides a sympathetic background to her incoherent thoughts.

Everything is a jumbled up, jumping around mess.

Emotions are stretched to breaking point.

Her name is Banafsha.

She is a journalist and supposed to be impartial.

The first time she left Afghanistan, on horseback over the Kurram Pass into Pakistan surrounded by hundreds of fleeing refugees she felt like one of them.

Was one of them.

Identified with them.

Belonged.

Felt like she was leaving home.

Felt that Afghanistan was home during the long years of separation which followed.

Now...she is not so sure.

The previous certainty has dissolved in the Central Asian melting pot of Kabul.

The people of her past are completely different than those of the present.

Memories turn into dreams, the dreams into a new, confusing reality.

She cannot yet make sense of it all.

The choking lump in her throat doesn't help.

The plane crosses the high mountain border into Pakistan leaving Banafsha on the other side.

Zahrah is the one who disembarks, collects her suitcase, picks up her life and heads for home.

Afghanistan, the time spent travelling in the mountains with the legendary *Mujahideen* is finally in the past.

Filed and gone.

Zahrah hears the echo of Anwar's voice in the departure lounge of Dalcross Airport, Inverness.

It echoes down through the long tunnel of years, whispers around the enclosed space of the yellow cab as it climbs the narrow, winding road towards Bhurban.

It rustles the night time pine trees, traces footprints in the wind as she makes her torchlight way down the steep mountain path which she climbed up a mere nine days before when things were different.

A large dog fox crosses the boulder strewn path.

A jackal howls at the moon.

A pack of hyenas answer.

The echo finally catches up.

'Time does not come twice,' he said.

The sharp scent of a predatory leopard lingers on the cold breeze which has suddenly sprung up from somewhere close at hand.

The danger is palpable.

A live thing.

She walks faster.

Eager for safety.

For security.

'Time does not come twice,' Anwar echoes insistently.

The truth hits like a hammer between her shoulder blades.

Leaves ice in the pit of her stomach.

He is right.

AFTERWORD

Conditions in Afghanistan have deteriorated rapidly since I was there, though many people, some governments included, would not agree with me on this point.

ISAF forces, accompanied by NATO troops, continue to menace the populace, intentionally or unintentionally as the case may be.

Cases of human rights abuse, torture of prisoners in occupation force jails, have come to international attention.

University students and villagers alike have held demonstrations against the presence of foreign troops on Afghan soil.

The *Taliban* have regained ground in many localities.

Suicide bombers have arrived on the scene.

Foreign aid workers, male and female, have been kidnapped, held for ransom or simply shot.

Some aid agencies have completely pulled out.

Atrocities, both human and economic, are on the increase.

The cauldron is simmering and quite likely to boil over in the not too distant future.

Elections have been held.

President Karzai has, under intense pressure, exchanged his American bodyguards for Afghan ones.

Anwar continues in his attempt at organizing unity.

Gulbuddin Hekmatyar has spoken out of his hiding place, proclaiming that no such unity is possible while foreign troops are present.

The number of foreign troops is set to increase yet again as they try to bring some form of peace to the country as a whole.

Kabul continues to exist as a predominantly separate entity to the rest of Afghanistan.

Farhad, as expected, returned to London, but surprisingly, his girl has gone with him.

I understand that, although they are still together, the *shadi* has not yet taken place.

In researching some material on Afghanistan I recently came across a report compiled by Dr Patricia Gossman for the Afghan Justice Project. The report, 'Casting Shadows: War Crimes and Crimes against Humanity' documents horrific abuses in Afghanistan from 1978 to 2001, detailing incidences and naming names of perpetrators on all sides of the conflict be they Russian, Afghan or otherwise. It makes for nightmare reading.

Amongst the names of *Mujahideen* commanders accused of human rights abuses are those of Ahmed Shah Massoud and numerous other 'respected' commanders. I read the report with more than a little trepidation. Mullah 'Izzat' or 'Ezzat', of the beautiful garden at Kargha, is high on the list of those recommended for prosecution as war criminals, as are the names of a sizeable number of people currently holding important government positions.

Much to my relief, the names of Commander Mohammad Anwar Jekdalek and Commander Gul Ruz are not included.

GLOSSARY

Abaya	An overgarment worn by some Muslim women.
Adda	Bus or truck stand.
Ashak	Leek filled steamed pasta square.
Aloo	Potato.
Baba	Old man.
Bhabi	Elder brother's wife.
Bhaijan	Elder brother.
Balay	Yes.
Bazaar	Market.
Bhalus	Bears.
Bhindi	Okra or Ladies Finger.
Burkha	Totally concealing garment with fine mesh at eye level in order to allow the wearer to see.
Buccha	Male child.
Chadar	Shawl.
Chappals	Open sandals.
Charpoy	Rope bed.
Chemise	Loose shirt.
Chai	Tea.
Chinar	Maple.
Chine	Chinese.
Chula	Stove.
Churis	Bangles.
Dari	Afghan dialect of Persian.
Desi	Rural, indigenous.
Dupatta	Ladies long scarf.
Gharara	Voluminous long skirt.
Gilam Jam	Carpet thieves.
Golis	Tablets, bullets.
Haveli	Fortress type house.
Henna	Powdered tree berries used in decorating body and for dying hair etc.
Hijab	Ladies head covering.
Itehad	Unity.
Jali	Fly screen.
Jan	Beloved, life.

Jang	War.
Jegdalek	A place in Afghanistan.
Jahez	Dowry.
Jekdalek	Afghan name.
Jihad	Holy war.
Jirga	Meeting of tribal elders.
Jora	Suit, a pair.
Kagazi Badam	Papery shelled almond.
Kameez	Loose fitting tunic/dress.
Khanum	Lady.
Kebab	Piece of grilled or fried meat.
Khargosh	Hare.
Kheer	Sweet milk pudding.
Khuda Hafiz	Goodbye.
Kish-mish	Raisons/sultanas.
Kofta	Meat ball.
Kuccha	Raw, basic.
Kukri	Curved dagger.
Kuli	Panel of cloth.
Kurash	Traditional Afghan wrestling.
Kurta	Loose fitting tunic/dress.
Lobia	Beans.
Mehman khana	Guest house.
Mali	Gardener.
Mantu	Steamed pasta square stuffed with minced lamb.
Maulvi/Mullah	Priest.
Motia	Jasmine.
Mujahid	Freedom fighter.
Mujahideen	Plural of Mujahid.
Namaz	Prayers.
Nan	Flat bread.
Paan	Sweet made of beetle nut and other ingredients.
Pakol	Flat woollen cap.
Peshmerga	Those ready to die.
Pilau	Rice dish.
Punkha	Fan.
Purdah	Private place or way of life for women.
Rishtadars	Relatives.
Russ	Russian.
Sabaz	Green.
Salen	Curry.
Sari	Indian ladies costume.

Shadi	Wedding.
Shalwar	Loose trousers.
Sherwara	A style of traditional Pakistani or Indian outfit.
Shirazi	Carpet from Shiraz in Iran.
Shoora	Council meeting.
Takht	Raised wooden seating/sleeping platform.
Talib	Religious student.
Taliban	Plural of Talib.
Tashakkor	Thank you.
Tor	Black.
Zanjeer	Chain.

BIBLIOGRAPHY

Ahmad, Colonel (retd) N.D., *The Survival of Afghanistan 1747-1979: The Historical Background of Afghan Crisis*, Institute of Islamic Culture, 1990.

Babur Padsha, Zahiru'd-din Muhammad, *Babur-Nama* (Memoirs of Babur), translated by Annette Susannah Beveridge, Munshiram Manoharlal Publishers Pvt. Ltd., New Delhi, 1998.

Buzzati, Dino, *The Tartar Steppe*, translated by Stuart C. Hood, Carcanet Press Limited, 1985.

Byron, Robert, *The Road to Oxiana*, Picador, 1981.

Dupree, Nancy Hatch, *An Historical Guide to Afghanistan*, Afghan Tourist Organization Publication Number 5, 1977.

Elliot, Major-General J.G., *The Frontier 1839–1947*, Cassell, 1968.

Ferrier, J.P., *Caravan Journeys and Wanderings in Persia, Afghanistan, Turkistan and Beloochistan*, Oxford University Press, 1976.

Fullerton, John, *The Soviet Occupation of Afghanistan*, Methuen, 1984.

Gossman, Dr Patricia, Report 'Casting Shadows: War Crimes and Crimes against Humanity', The Afghan Justice Project, 2005.

Harrison, Selig S., *In Afghanistan's Shadow: Baluch Nationalism and Soviet Temptations*, Carnegie Endowment for International Peace, 1981.

Hosseini, Khaled, *The Kite Runner*, Bloomsbury, 2003.

Hussain, Syed Shabbir; Alvi, Abdul Hamid; Rizvi, Absar Hussain, *Afghanistan Under Soviet Occupation*, World Affairs Publications, 1980.

Kaplan, Robert, *Soldiers of God: With Islamic Warriors in Afghanistan and Pakistan*, Vintage Departures, 2001.

Khayyam, Omar, *Rubaiyat*, translated by Edward Fitzgerald, Collins, 1974.

Kremmer, Christopher, *The Carpet Wars: From Kabul to Baghdad: A Ten-Year Journey Along Ancient Trade Routes*, Harper Collins, 2002.

Latifa, *My Forbidden Face: Growing Up Under the Taliban*, in collaboration with Shekeba Hachemi, translated by Linda Coverdale, talk Miramax books, 2001.

Levi, Peter, *The Light Garden of the Angel King*, Collins, 1972.

Macintyre, Ben, *The Man Who Would Be King: The First American in Afghanistan*, Farrar Straus Giroux, 2004.

Medley, Dominic and Barrand, Jude, *The Survival Guide to Kabul: The Bradt Mini Guide*, Bradt Travel Guides Ltd., UK & The Globe Pequot Press inc, USA, 2003.

Michener, James, *Caravans*, Martin Secker & Warburg, 1964.

Palmer, Louis, *Adventures in Afghanistan*, Octagon Press, 1990.

Shah, Safia (ed.), *Afghan Caravan*, Octagon Press, 1990.

Shakib, Siba, *Samira and Samir*, Century, 2004.

Wilson, Andrew, *North from Kabul*, George Allen & Unwin Ltd., 1961.